Moodle Security

Learn how to install and configure Moodle in the most secure way possible

Darko Miletić

BIRMINGHAM - MUMBAI

Moodle Security

First published: February 2011

Production Reference: 1070211

Published by Packt Publishing Ltd.
32 Lincoln Road
Olton
Birmingham, B27 6PA, UK.

ISBN 978-1-849512-64-0

www.packtpub.com

Cover Image by Asher Wishkerman (a.wishkerman@mpic.de)

Credits

Author
Darko Miletić

Reviewers
Mary Cooch
Ângelo Marcos Rigo
Susan Smith Nash

Acquisition Editor
Sarah Cullington

Development Editor
Neha Mallik

Technical Editor
Pallavi Kachare

Indexer
Hemangini Bari

Editorial Team Leader
Aanchal Kumar

Project Team Leader
Ashwin Shetty

Project Coordinator
Poorvi Nair

Proofreader
Lynda Sliwoski

Production Coordinator
Melwyn D'Sa

Cover Work
Melwyn D'Sa

About the Author

Darko Miletić has been enchanted by computers ever since he saw ZX Spectrum 48K back in 1985. From that moment his only goal was to learn as much as possible about these new contraptions. That dedication eventually led him to work as a part of the editorial staff of Serbian computer magazine "Personalni Računari" where he had a regular column about Microsoft Office. At the same time he studied Mechanical Engineering at the Belgrade University but decided he liked designing computer programs more than designing machines. In 2004, he moved to Argentina and soon started working with e-learning using various web technologies and, as of 2008, his focus is entirely on the Open Source Learning Management System, Moodle. He also led the development of IMS Common Cartridge v1 support for Moodle (1.9 and 2) which is now part of standard Moodle release. Currently, he is working as chief software architect in at Loom Inc. where he leads the development of Loom.

Loom is the Managed Open Source LMS developed specifically to provide a personalized, comprehensive, e-learning experience. It merges the benefits of Open Source technology with the reliability of enterprise support, the dynamic scaling of cloud hosting, and power of customization. It offers complete services including content development, implementation management, faculty and administrative training, and custom programming needs. It is dedicated to developing products and services such as Weaver that are focused on utilizing the data with the LMS to support student retention, to facilitate faculty performance, and to bring about learning outcomes that maximize the success and satisfaction of our clients.

In his spare time, Darko tries to promote electronic books, works on few open source projects, translates SF stories from Serbian to Spanish, and reads a lot.

Writing this book was not a simple task and I would like to thank all the people who helped me write it. First and foremost my thanks goes to Dr. Dietrichson, who had the patience to read and modify some parts of the text and to all the good folks at Loom and UVCMS. Many thanks to my wife who exercised a lot of patience. Thanks to Gustavo Cerati, Sting, Rambo Amadeus, Habib Koité, and *The Doors* who made this journey much more smooth and pleasant with their music.

About the Reviewers

Mary Cooch is the author of *Moodle 2.0 First Look* and *Moodle 1.9 For Teaching 7-14 Year Olds*, both published by Packt. A teacher for 25 years, Mary is based at Our Lady's High School Preston, Lancashire, UK but now spends part of her working week traveling Europe and showing others how to make the most of this popular Virtual Learning Environment. Known online as moodlefairy, Mary runs a blog on www.moodleblog.org and may be contacted for consultation on mco@olchs.lancs.sch.uk.

Ângelo Marcos Rigo is a 34 years-old web developer who has enjoyed creating customization and fixing web systems since the launching of the Internet in Brasil in 1995.

He has experience with languages PHP, ASP, JSP, Asp.net, ZOPE, and with the following databases: Mysql, Postgresql, Oracle, MSSql.

He has worked in the past for companies in the field of Telecom, for Primary Education, State Departments and also in the PUCRS faculty for the CEAD Department of Distance Learning.

I would like to thank my wife Janaína and daughter Lorena for their support, and for understanding how reviewing is fascinating.

Susan Smith Nash, is currently the Director of Education and Professional Development for the American Association of Petroleum Geologists (AAPG) in Tulsa, Oklahoma, and an adjunct professor at The University of Oklahoma. She was an associate dean for graduate programs at Excelsior College (Albany, NY). Previous to that, she was online courses manager at the Institute for Exploration and Development Geosciences, and director of curriculum development for the College of Liberal Studies at the University of Oklahoma, Norman, US, where she developed degree program curriculum for online courses at the university. She also developed an interface for courses as well as administrative and procedural support, support programmers, protocol and training manuals, and marketing approaches. She obtained her Ph.D. and M.A. in English and a B.S. in Geology from the University of Oklahoma. Nash blogs at E-Learning Queen (http://www.elearningqueen.com) and E-Learners (http://www.elearner.com), and has written articles and chapters on mobile learning, poetics, contemporary culture, and e-learning for numerous publications, including *Trends and issues in instructional design and technology (3rd ed)*, *Mobile Information Communication Technologies Adoption in Developing Countries: Effects and Implications, Talisman, Press1, International Journal of Learning Objects, GHR, World Literature,* and *Gargoyle*. Her latest books include *Moodle 1.9 Teaching Techniques* (Packt Publishing, 2010), *E-Learners Survival Guide* (Texture Press, 2009), and *Klub Dobrih Dejanj* (2008).

I'd like to express my appreciation to Poorvi Nair for demonstrating the highest level of professionalism and project guidance.

www.PacktPub.com

Support files, eBooks, discount offers and more

You might want to visit www.PacktPub.com for support files and downloads related to your book.

Did you know that Packt offers eBook versions of every book published, with PDF and ePub files available? You can upgrade to the eBook version at www.PacktPub.com and as a print book customer, you are entitled to a discount on the eBook copy. Get in touch with us at service@packtpub.com for more details.

At www.PacktPub.com, you can also read a collection of free technical articles, sign up for a range of free newsletters and receive exclusive discounts and offers on Packt books and eBooks.

http://PacktLib.PacktPub.com

Do you need instant solutions to your IT questions? PacktLib is Packt's online digital book library. Here, you can access, read, and search across Packt's entire library of books.

Why Subscribe?

- Fully searchable across every book published by Packt
- Copy and paste, print and bookmark content
- On demand and accessible via web browser

Free Access for Packt account holders

If you have an account with Packt at www.PacktPub.com, you can use this to access PacktLib today and view nine entirely free books. Simply use your login credentials for immediate access.

Table of Contents

Preface

Moving your classes and resources online with a Learning Management System such as Moodle opens up a whole world of possibilities for teaching your students. However, it also opens up a number of threats as your students, private information, and resources become vulnerable to cyber attacks. Learn how to safeguard Moodle to keep the bad guys at bay.

Moodle Security will show you how to make sure that only authorized users can access the information on your Moodle site. This may seem simple, but every day, systems get hacked and information gets lost or misused. Imagine the consequences if that were to happen in your school. The straightforward examples in this book will help you to lock down those access routes one door at a time.

By learning about the different types of potential threats, reading this book will prepare you for the worst. Web robots can harvest your e-mail addresses to send spam e-mails from your account, which could have devastating effects. Moodle comes with a number of set roles and permissions—make sure these are assigned to the right people, and are set to keep out the spam bots, using Moodle's authentication features. Learn how to secure both Windows and Linux servers and to make sure that none of your system files are accessible to the wrong people. Many of the most dangerous web attacks come from inside your system, so once you have all of your security settings in place, you will learn to monitor user activity to make sure that there are no threats from registered users. You will learn to work with the tools that help you to do this and enable you to back up your settings so that even a crashed system can't bother you.

What this book covers

Chapter 1, Delving into World of Security opens the book with a basic introduction regarding the importance of security in web-based systems with total emphasis on Moodle. We expose weak points in every Moodle installation and offer a quick procedure for securely installing a new or securing an existing Moodle instance.

Chapter 2, Securing your server – Linux covers everything that helps securing typical Linux server starting with the OS basics and then moving on a web server configuration, PHP configuration, and database server configuration. Reader will be presented with a detailed explanation regarding inner workings of the file system on Linux and is offered a concrete examples on how to best utilize them regarding Moodle setup. If you do not use or plan on using Linux-based server for your Moodle setup you can skip this chapter.

Chapter 3, Securing your server – Windows covers the general subject of installing basic pieces needed for running Moodle and securing them on a server with Windows OS. We start with the basics related to the general OS issues and then offer explanation regarding file security and ways of getting, deploying, and securing Moodle files. Readers will also be presented with recommended installation and configuration process of PHP under Windows web server and recommended installation and configuration of MySQL.

Chapter 4, Authentication is dedicated to the topic of authentication. What it is and the way it is implemented in Moodle. We present the most used authentication methods and the detailed explanation regarding potential security issues and ways of handling them.

Chapter 5, Roles and Permissions explains that every complex system offers various usage patterns based on user needs and obligations. Based on such use cases we can identify specific roles. Moodle is no different in this respect. By assigning users to one of the predefined or custom roles we are defining spectrum of the options and actions available to them at every location within LMS. It is paramount for every administrator to understand the access rights as they are implemented. Therefore, in this chapter we will focus on access rights to resources and functions within Moodle starting with Roles and Capabilities, Standard Roles, ways of customizing roles, and our take on best practices regarding roles.

Chapter 6, Protection against bots explains how with search engines we – the common users, can find almost anything that is of our personal interest but as a website owner and/or administrator we must know what amount of information is available to the general public and if that amount surpasses our intention or allow boundaries, then we must know how to detect such case and remedy the situation. In this chapter we will dedicate to the exposing the danger of Internet bots. What they are and how they work and how to combat against them.

Chapter 7, Securing user files speaks about potential dangers that can be introduced into Moodle by the users. We list all points where one user can upload a custom file. How that file can affect other users (virus infection, inappropriate content, etc.). What can we do to protect our system and other users against these undesired introductions into system. We also explain in detail how to install, configure, and integrate ClamAV anti-virus in Moodle.

Chapter 8, Securing Moodle Data explains that when we talk about Moodle data we are referring to both user and course information that is within the platform. In the previous chapter we were talking about user files only. Now we will focus our attention to the protection and separation of internal Moodle data between valid platform users. The topics we will cover are user information protection, course information protection, and best practices for using and applying the techniques presented.

Chapter 9, Monitoring User Activity explains that an administrator's work does not end with installation and configuration of Moodle and an operating system. He should constantly monitor the server state and react as quickly as possible. In this chapter we will talk about ways of monitoring the status of Moodle and underlying OS components. We offer list of tools and utilities that can be used on both Linux and Windows for performing these tasks and also a separate section that deals with reports and other elements offered by Moodle for monitoring system activity. We explain how to set up and configure Google maps with Moodle, how to configure Moodle cron and how to configure and use statistics report. The reader is also offered a detailed step by step guide to setting up Webalizer—web traffic analyzer.

Chapter 10, Backup is the cornerstone of every well maintained production server. This chapter will try to explain the importance of such procedures regarding Moodle and present tools available both within the platform and outside of it. We will also try to offer some guidelines for what to do in case of total server failure. The reader will be presented with scripts for Linux and Windows that can be used for performing reliable backup procedures.

Appendix offers a list of less used authentication plugins within Moodle, with their short description and potential uses.

Who this book is for

If you are in charge of Moodle—whether you are an administrator or lead teacher—then securing it is one of the most important things that you can do. You need to know the basics of working with Moodle, but no previous experience of system administration is required.

Conventions

In this book, you will find a number of styles of text that distinguish between different kinds of information. Here are some examples of these styles, and an explanation of their meaning.

Code words in text are shown as follows: "Create a directory called `moodledata` somewhere on the disk."

A block of code is set as follows:

```
DatabaseDirectory Z:\clamav\db
DatabaseMirror clamav.edebris.com
DatabaseMirror database.clamav.net
NotifyClamd Z:\clamav\clamd.conf
```

Any command-line input or output is written as follows:

```
CREATE DATABASE moodle CHARSET 'utf8' COLLATION 'utf8_general_ci';

CREATE USER 'moodle'@'localhost' IDENTIFIED BY 'somepass';
```

New terms and **important words** are shown in bold. Words that you see on the screen, in menus or dialog boxes for example, appear in the text like this: "Make sure you check **Unattended operation** at the bottom".

 Warnings or important notes appear in a box like this.

Reader feedback

Feedback from our readers is always welcome. Let us know what you think about this book—what you liked or may have disliked. Reader feedback is important for us to develop titles that you really get the most out of.

To send us general feedback, simply send an e-mail to feedback@packtpub.com, and mention the book title via the subject of your message.

If there is a book that you need and would like to see us publish, please send us a note in the **SUGGEST A TITLE** form on www.packtpub.com or e-mail suggest@packtpub.com.

If there is a topic that you have expertise in and you are interested in either writing or contributing to a book, see our author guide on www.packtpub.com/authors.

Customer support

Now that you are the proud owner of a Packt book, we have a number of things to help you to get the most from your purchase.

> **Downloading the example code for this book**
>
> You can download the example code files for all Packt books you have purchased from your account at http://www.PacktPub.com. If you purchased this book elsewhere, you can visit http://www.PacktPub.com/support and register to have the files e-mailed directly to you.

Errata

Although we have taken every care to ensure the accuracy of our content, mistakes do happen. If you find a mistake in one of our books—maybe a mistake in the text or the code—we would be grateful if you would report this to us. By doing so, you can save other readers from frustration and help us improve subsequent versions of this book. If you find any errata, please report them by visiting http://www.packtpub.com/support, selecting your book, clicking on the **errata submission form** link, and entering the details of your errata. Once your errata are verified, your submission will be accepted and the errata will be uploaded on our website, or added to any list of existing errata, under the Errata section of that title. Any existing errata can be viewed by selecting your title from http://www.packtpub.com/support.

Piracy

Piracy of copyright material on the Internet is an ongoing problem across all media. At Packt, we take the protection of our copyright and licenses very seriously. If you come across any illegal copies of our works, in any form, on the Internet, please provide us with the location address or website name immediately so that we can pursue a remedy.

Please contact us at copyright@packtpub.com with a link to the suspected pirated material.

We appreciate your help in protecting our authors, and our ability to bring you valuable content.

Questions

You can contact us at questions@packtpub.com if you are having a problem with any aspect of the book, and we will do our best to address it.

Delving into the World of Security

1

Welcome to Moodle Security!

In the early days of the web, Internet was mostly used for academic purposes. Hence, all communications protocols had very little or no focus on security. The situation started changing as more and more public and commercial services started moving online and common users started actually using Internet in their daily routine. With the increase of user base we see the emerge of the malicious groups of users, the so-called hackers that are focused mostly on information theft and illegal usage. Nowadays it is quite common to be attacked by hacker(s). In fact it is so common and frequent that it is reported that only the USA's cyber attacks generate costs up to 10 billion dollars every year. The purpose of this book is to introduce you to web security while focusing on Moodle.

In this chapter we will cover the following topics:

- Moodle and security
- Weak points
- The secure Moodle installation
- Quickly securing Moodle

Moodle and security

Moodle is an open source **CMS (Course Management System)/LMS (Learning Management System)/VLE (Virtual Learning Environment)**. Its primary purpose is to enable educational institutions and individuals to create and publish learning content in a coherent and pedagogically valuable manner, so that it can be used for successful knowledge transfer towards students.

That sounds harmless enough. Why would anybody want to illegally access an educational platform?

There are various motives of computer criminals. In general, they are people committed to the circumvention of computer security. This primarily concerns unauthorized remote computer break-ins via a communication network such as the Internet. Some of the motives could be:

- **Financial**: Stealing user and/or course information and selling it to other third-parties
- **Personal**: Personal grudge, infantile display of power, desire to alter assigned grades, and so on

Weak points

Moodle is a web application and as such must be hosted on a computer connected to some kind of network (private or public—Internet / Intranet). This computer must have the following components:

- Operating System (OS)
- Web server
- PHP
- Database server
- Moodle

Each of these pieces can be used as a point of attack by a malicious user(s) in order to obtain access to the protected information. Therefore, it is our task to make all of them as secure as possible. The main focus will be directed towards our Moodle and PHP configuration. At the end of the book you can find some recommended literature for additional reading.

The secure installation of Moodle

In this section we follow a secure installation of Moodle. In case you do not already have an installed instance of Moodle, we will show you the quickest way to do that, and at the same time focus on security. If you already have Moodle installed, go to the following section where you will see how to secure an existing installation of Moodle.

Starting from scratch

In order to install Moodle on your server you need to install and configure the web server with support for PHP and the database server. We will not go into the specifics of setting up a particular web server, PHP, and/or database server right now, since it depends on the OS your server has installed. Also we will not explain in detail tasks like creating directories, setting up file permissions, etc as they are OS specific. Later in this book we will address them in detail for both Linux and Windows. If you need to know that right now then I suggest you go directly to the chapter dedicated to the Operating System you plan on using. This section assumes you already know about your OS and have already configured your web server with an empty database. Every installation of Moodle must have:

- Web server with PHP support
- Dedicated database
- Two dedicated directories — one for Moodle and another for platform data

 We assume that your web server is Apache (Linux) or IIS (Windows), and that you use PHP 5.1.x or later and MySQL 5.0 or later.

Installation checklist

The following checklist will guide you through the basic installation procedure for Moodle.

1. Download the latest stable version of Moodle from `http://download.moodle.org/`. (At the time of writing this book it is 1.9.8+). You have two options available on the download page—`moodle-weekly-19.tgz` or `moodle-weekly-19.zip` archive. In case you use Linux you can choose either. In case of Windows, ZIP file is the preferred choice. The reason for this is simple. Every Windows server comes, by default, with installed support for managing Zip archives. On the other hand, TGZ is readily available on every Linux distribution.

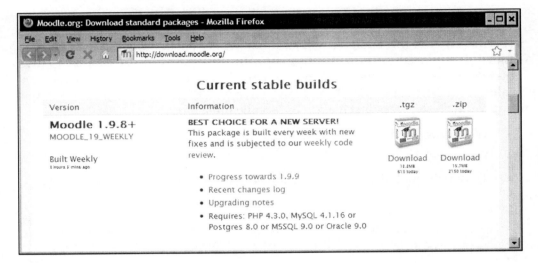

2. Unpack the compressed file you just downloaded. This will produce a directory with the name `moodle` which contains all of the platform files. Move that directory to the web-root of your web server. After doing that it is recommended to make all files read-only for safety reasons.

3. Create a directory called `moodledata` somewhere on the disk. Make sure that it is not in the web-root of your web server since that would incur a serious security breach. Doing that might expose all platform files submitted by course participants and teachers together with the course content to the outside world.

4. Create an empty database (we suggest the name moodle or moodledb).
    The default database character set must be configured to utf8 and collation
    set to utf8_general_ci. It is recommended to have a special user for
    accessing this database with limited permissions. In case of credentials theft,
    a malicious user could only operate on data from one database, minimizing
    the potential damage. That database user account will need permissions for
    creating, altering, and deleting the tables, creating/dropping the indexes and
    reading/writing the data. Here is what you need to execute in your MySQL
    console for creating a database and user:

    ```
    CREATE DATABASE moodle CHARSET 'utf8' COLLATION 'utf8_general_
    ci';

    CREATE USER 'moodle'@'localhost' IDENTIFIED BY 'somepass';

    GRANT SELECT, INSERT, UPDATE, DELETE, CREATE, DROP, INDEX, ALTER
    ON loomdb.\* TO loom@localhost IDENTIFIED BY 'somepass';

    FLUSH PRIVILEGES;
    ```

5. Start the installation by opening the http://<url to local installation
    of the moodle> (for example http://localhost/moodle) in your browser.
    Make sure it is a more recent browser with pop ups and JavaScript enabled.
    We recommend Internet Explorer 8+ or Firefox 3.6+. You will see the
    following screenshot:

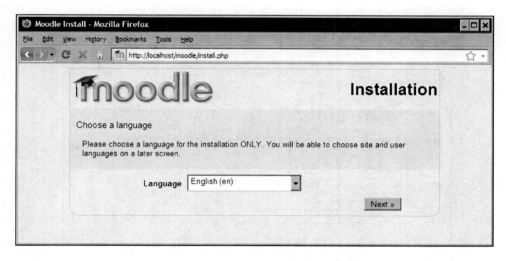

6. On the next screen, we need to specify the web address of the platform and the location of the moodle directory on the disk.

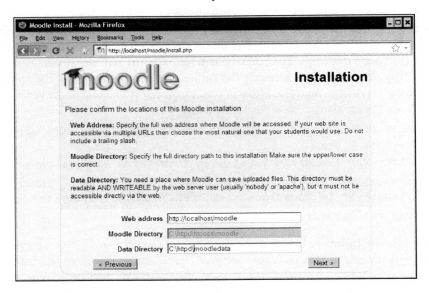

7. Now, we must configure database access. Choose MySQL as database type, localhost as host server, set the name of the database (moodle), database user, and its password (moodle/moodle). You should leave the table prefix as is.

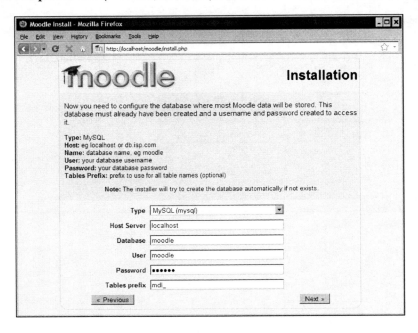

8. Moodle checks the server configuration on this screen and displays the outcome. We can proceed with the installation only if all of the minimal requirements are met.

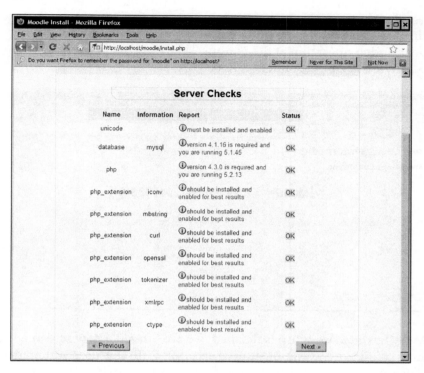

9. During installation, Moodle generates a configuration file within the moodle directory called `config.php`. It is important to make this file read-only after installation for security reasons. In case Moodle cannot save `config.php` it will offer to download or copy content of the file and manually place it in the appropriate location on the server. See the following screenshot:

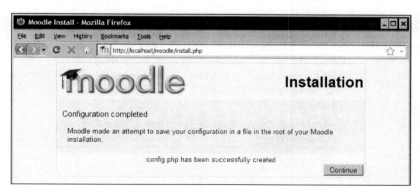

10. We are now presented with terms of usage and license agreement. To proceed click **yes**.

11. We can now start the installation itself. During that process Moodle will create all of the tables in the database, session files in the moodledata directory, and load some initial information. Make sure you check **Unattended operation** at the bottom. That way, the process will be executed without user intervention.

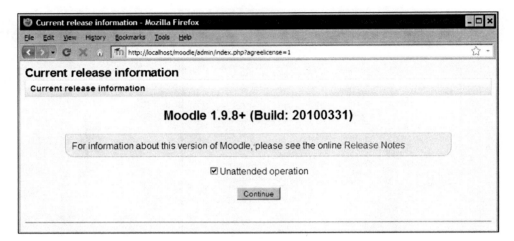

12. After the database setup is finished, we are offered a new screen where we must configure the administrative account. With this user you manage your platform, so be careful about disclosing this information to other users.

Field name	Description	Recommended action
Username	Defines user name inside the Moodle. By default it is admin.	We recommend leaving the default value unchanged.
New password	Defines user logon password.	Must supply valid password.
First name	Defines name of the admin.	Must supply valid name.
Surname	Defines surname of the admin.	Must supply valid name.
E-mail address	Defines user e-mail address.	Must supply valid e-mail.
E-mail display	Define the visibility of your e-mail address within the platform.	We recommend leaving it as is (visible to all).
E-mail active	Defines whether e-mail is activated or not.	Set it to enable.

Field name	Description	Recommended action
City/Town	Defines name of the city where you live.	Moodle requires this value.
Select Country	Name of your country.	Set it to your country name.
Timezone	Sets your time zone so that server can display time calculated for your location in some reports.	If not sure what your time zone is, leave it as is.
Preferred language	Choose the platform language.	By default, Moodle comes only with support for English language. If you want to add more languages visit `http://download.moodle.org/lang16/` and download and install the appropriate files.

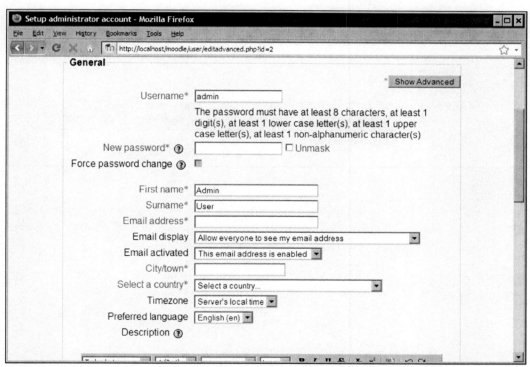

13. After configuring administrative user there is just one more step to complete and that is setting up the site title and short name. In the **Full site name** field, place the long name you would like to set for your website; it can have multiple words. In the **Short name for the site** field put one word without spaces which will represent your website. In the **Front Page Description** field put a longer description (one paragraph) that explains in more detail the purpose of your site. This is optional and does not affect the Moodle functionality at all.

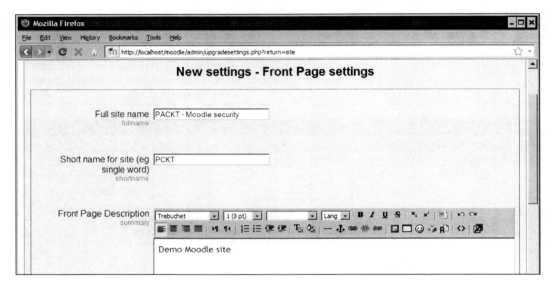

14. You have now finished installing Moodle and should see the following screenshot:

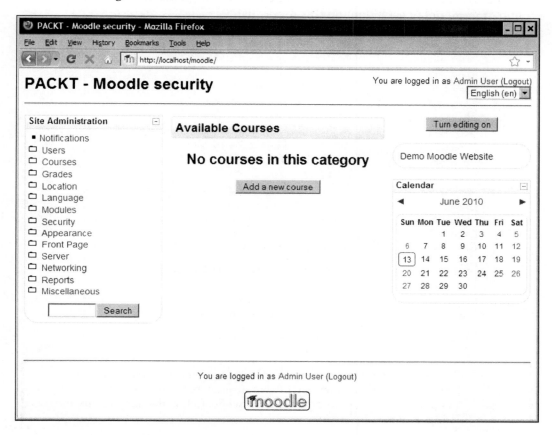

Quickly securing Moodle

Moodle offers a quick way of detecting major security issues within your platform setup and that is the security overview report. Go to the **Reports | Security** overview page. A well configured Moodle should display the following screenshot. In case there are discrepancies, then review the explication near each issue that displays a warning and take the appropriate actions.

Right now, we will give you a simple what to do list in order to pass the security check report without going into too much details. Throughout this book, we will explain in more detail each item on this report list.

Register globals	OK	Register globals are disabled.
Insecure dataroot	OK	Dataroot directory must not be accessible via the web.
Displaying of PHP errors	OK	Displaying of PHP errors disabled.
No authentication	OK	No authentication plugin is disabled.
Allow EMBED and OBJECT	OK	Unlimited object embedding is not allowed.
Enabled .swf media filter	OK	Flash media filter is not enabled.
Open user profiles	OK	Login is required before viewing user profiles.
Open to Google	OK	Search engine access is not enabled.
Password policy	OK	Password policy enabled.
Password salt	OK	Password salt is OK
Email change confirmation	OK	Confirmation of change of email address in user profile.
Writable config.php	Warning	PHP scripts may modify config.php.
XSS trusted users	Warning	RISK_XSS - found 1 users that have to be trusted.
Administrators	OK	Found 1 server administrator(s).
Backup of user data	Warning	Found 1 roles, 0 overrides and 1 users with the ability to backup user data.
Default role for all users	OK	Default role for all users definition is OK.
Guest role	OK	Guest role definition is OK.
Frontpage role	Information	Frontpage role is not set.
Default course role (global)	OK	Site default role definition is OK
Default roles (courses)	OK	Used only default course role

The security overview report is available starting from Moodle 1.8.9 and 1.9.4. If you have an older version we strongly recommend you perform an upgrade to a more recent one. Meanwhile, follow the instructions and configure your LMS as suggested.

The checklist in security overview report consists of items that compare current configuration of your system with the recommended one and report the status. Some of the items in the checklist apply to the PHP configuration and others apply to the Moodle configuration.

PHP is configured through a special file called `php.ini`. The location of this file may vary depending on your OS and type of installation. On Linux it may be usually found at `/etc/php.ini`. To modify this file you can use any text editor available (vi, nano, notepad, etc.).

After every modification of `php.ini` you must restart your web server so that the changes may be applied to the system.

Moodle can be configured by using the configuration pages in the administrative part of the platform or by modification of a special configuration file called `config.php`. Some configuration options are exclusive to the `config.php` file while others are exclusive to administration interface.

Review the Moodle security overview report

We will now go through every option in the security overview report and explain briefly what it means together with the actual steps you need to perform in order to remedy potential security flaw.

- **Register Globals**: This is a PHP setting that can be configured by modifying the PHP configuration file—`php.ini`. This is the default setting in PHP since version 4.2. Make sure you have the following line in your `php.ini`:

  ```
  register_globals = Off
  ```

- **Insecure dataroot**: If the status for this item is not OK it means that the `moodledata` folder is placed in a location accessible from the Web without any protection. The solution to this is either to move this folder to some other location or prevent public access with the appropriate web server configuration. For example, if your Moodle is located in `/var/www/html/moodle` and your `moodledata` is located in `/var/www/html/moodledata` the report will show this as an error. To fix this you need to change the location of moodledata to some other directory, for example to `/var/www/moodledata`.

- **Displaying PHP errors** (`display_errors` option): The `display_errors` directive determines whether error messages generated by PHP code should be sent to the browser. These messages frequently contain sensitive information about your web application environment, and should never be presented to mistrusted sources. Make sure it is configured like this in your `php.ini`:

  ```
  display_errors = Off
  ```

- **No authentication**: It is a Moodle configuration option. Make sure the "No authentication" plugin is disabled. Go to **Administration | Users | Authentication | Manage authentication** and configure it as displayed in the following screenshot:

Active authentication plugins

Name	Enable	Up/Down	Settings
Manual accounts			Settings
No login			Settings
Email-based self-registration	👁		Settings
CAS server (SSO)	⌄		Settings
External database	⌄		Settings
FirstClass server	⌄		Settings
IMAP server	⌄		Settings
LDAP server	⌄		Settings
Moodle Network authentication	⌄		Settings
NNTP server	⌄		Settings
No authentication	⌄		Settings
PAM (Pluggable Authentication Modules)	⌄		Settings
POP3 server	⌄		Settings
RADIUS server	⌄		Settings
Shibboleth	⌄		Settings

Please choose the authentication plugins you wish to use and arrange them in order of failthrough. Changes in table above are saved automatically.

- **Allow** EMBED **and** OBJECT: A Moodle configuration option. Go to **Administration | Security | Site policies** in your Moodle and make sure that the option **Allow EMBED and OBJECT tags** is not checked. EMBED and OBJECT tags are used for inserting third-party web browser plug ins for reproducing multimedia content (Adobe Flash, Apple QuickTime, etc.) or for running special embedded applications like java-applets. Some of these plug ins have well-known security issues and therefore are not recommended for general public usage. By disabling this option we are preventing users to add these elements to their pages or other generated content or responses.

- **Enabled** `.swf` **media filter**: Moodle configuration option. This should be disabled on production websites. Visit **Administration | Modules | Filters | Multimedia Plugins** and make sure it is disabled. This filter transforms any link to the Adobe Flash file to playable content by using integrated flash player. Since Flash has security issues this option is best left disabled.

- **Open user profiles**: Moodle configuration option. Checks if user public profiles are open to anybody. Best practice is to require login before permitting somebody to actually take a look into other people's personal information. Go to **Administration | Security | Site** policies and make sure **Force users to login for profiles** is checked.

- **Open to Google**: Moodle configuration option. Visit the Site policies page and uncheck **Open to Google**. With this option we choose whether we permit Google robots to scan the site's content and index it thereby permitting anybody to perform free-text search. In general, this is not a desired behavior in an LMS.

- **Password policy**: A password policy is a set of rules designed to enhance computer security by encouraging users to employ strong passwords and use them properly. On the Site policies page check **Password Policy**. By enabling this we enforce usage of "strong" passwords therefore making it impossible to use dictionary attacks.

- **Password salt**: Moodle stores encrypted versions of user passwords into database. Up until Moodle 1.9.8 it used the default way of encrypting user passwords which is prone to dictionary attacks. Password salt increases security of the generated encrypted passwords making a dictionary attack virtually impossible. As of Moodle 1.9.8 use of password salt is enabled by default. However, if you have an older version you can enable this by modifying the `config.php` file. Place something like this in your Moodle `config.php`:

```
$CFG->passwordsaltmain = '<randomly generated string>';
```

 Be aware that enabling password salt is only possible by editing `config.php`. You can generate good password salt by going to the special page designed for that purpose—`http://dev.moodle.org/gensalt.php`.

- **E-mail change confirmation**: Go to the Site policies page and enable **E-mail change confirmation**. Every user in Moodle must have a valid e-mail address. A common way of fiddling with somebody's personal account is to change his password and registered mail address. To prevent these situations we enable e-mail change confirmation which forces a user to confirm changed e-mail address. This is done through a special e-mail sent to the new account.

- **Writable** `config.php`: Make `config.php` read-only. For example, on Linux you would do something like this:

  ```
  chmod ug=r,o= <Moodle path>/config.php
  ```

- **XSS trusted users**: Moodle has a set of seven standard roles. By default, any user with Administrative role on the platform level is completely trusted. Be very careful about which users can have this role. Keep it to a smallest possible group.

- **Administrators**: Platform must have at least one user with Administrative role. By default that is user admin.

- **Backup of user data**: User data are something very sensitive for every educational institution. Under the **Family Educational Rights and Privacy Act (FERPA)** student information can be disclosed only to limited set of people directly related with either student's family or educational institution. Only very limited group of people should be able to export student information tied to a course.

- **Default role for all users**: This should be set to **Authenticated user**. If not go to **Administration | Users | Permissions | User policies** and configure it appropriately.

- **Guest role**: This should be set to Guest.

- **Frontpage role**: By default it is not set. You can leave it that way or create a special non-legacy role.

- **Default course role (global)**: The default setting for this is student. This is something that should seldom be changed.

- **Default course role**: Same thing as the previous one but on the course level. Again the default value here is student.

Summary

The World Wide Web is an entire universe filled with great opportunities but also a place with various threats to the normal operation and security of any website. In this chapter we provided a brief overview emphasizing the importance of security in a cyber universe. We learned the basic facts about the secure installation of Moodle and how to quickly make our existing Moodle instance more secure. This, of course, is not all. It is just the tip of the iceberg.

In the following chapters we will focus our attention to all of the fine details of properly configuring and optimizing a Moodle instance and all of the accompanying software.

Next stop—how to transform your server into an impenetrable fortress!

2
Securing Your Server – Linux

Linux has become a very important player as a mainstream operating system for servers. According to the Netcraft report of most reliable hosting company sites dating from February 2010, 6 out of 10 servers were running some brand of Linux. This indicates the strong position of this **Operating System (OS)** and the confidence it generates. Some of the reasons for this are:

- **Initial price**: Linux is open source and therefore free for commercial use
- **Stability and Reliability**: Linux is a highly stable and reliable platform with all of its elements well tested; any bug is usually quickly resolved by the community
- **Security**: Linux is, by default, quite secure and is in fact in a much better position than Windows since it is at risk from much fewer viruses and Trojans
- Better utilization of hardware resources
- Availability of commercial support

Another reason for which we are starting with Linux is because Moodle is primarily developed on Linux using MySQL, Apache and PHP, also MySQL (at least until version 5.5) is vastly superior on Linux.

In this chapter we will cover the following topics:

- Securing your Linux — the basics
- Apache configuration
- PHP configuration
- MySQL configuration
- File security permissions

Securing your Linux—the basics

We will try to explain the basic elements of Linux on which you should focus your attention during initial configuration.

Firewall

A Firewall is a part of a computer system designed to block or permit network communication based on set of predefined rules. The design and operation of the Internet is based on the Internet Protocol Suite, also commonly called Transfer Control Protocol / Internet Protocol (TCP/IP). In this system, hosts and host services are referenced using two components: an address and a port number. For example, HTTP—standard web protocol uses port 80 by default. In general, most services use a limited number of ports. A common technique for detecting running services on a public server is port scanning. It is used by administrators for verification of their security policies and by hackers for obtaining lists of potential targets for later attack. To prevent this and other types of misuse we should block access to all ports except the ones we want to expose to the public. This blocking is done by firewalls. They can be available either as hardware appliances or software service running on the server.

In this chapter and throughout this book, any practical examples offered for Linux apply to CentOS 5 Linux, which is an open source version of Red Hat Enterprise Linux 5 server. Firewall comes as standard in the out of the box product, so we will first show how to enable and configure it for safer functioning of our Moodle server.

1. Open the command line prompt, logon as the root to your server and execute **command setup**.

2. In the following screenshot we have several options for configuring various system services.

 We use command line utilities as they are faster and do not require installation of X server, which is usually unnecessary on server installations.

3. Select **Firewall configuration** option.

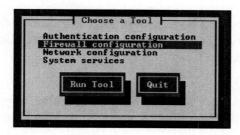

4. On the firewall page we can see the following options:

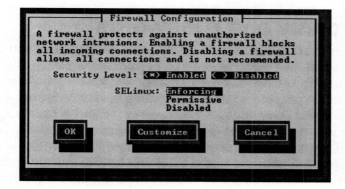

5. Set firewall to **Enabled**, but keep in mind that it will block all incoming connections from the Internet. This is too secure for our use case as we actually need to open a few ports. For this, we need to customize a further Firewall configuration.

6. Choose **Customize** options from the dialog to enter into the firewall customization section.

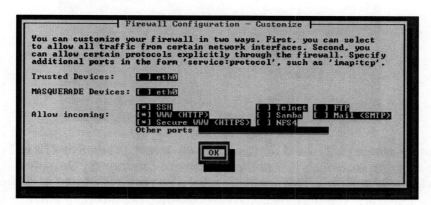

As you can see, we have selected the **SSH**, **WWW**, and **Secure WWW** options. These three are what are usually needed to have properly exposed web-server service. SSH service is enabled because it offers a standard access for remote administration of the server. In case you have another way of configuring your server, you can disable SSH.

 If your server is hosted by third-party hosting company, you will probably have an option to rent a firewall appliance box. I advise you to get it if it fits within your budget constraints. It is a much more robust way of protecting network access to your machine.

User accounts and passwords

In the 1983 movie "WarGames" there is a very characteristic scene with a young Matthew Broderick. In that scene we see him in front of the principal's office waiting for his meeting. On his left side there is an empty seat with a computer terminal linked to the school's computer system. As a young hacker he is keen on entering into the system without being noticed. The curse of forbidden fruit is again at work. In order to enter into the system he needs a valid password. Knowing how people hate remembering passwords, he assumes that it is probably written somewhere near the terminal so that whoever works there will be able to login without too much hassle. He opens a bottom drawer and voila! A piece of paper is glued to the drawer with the latest passwords, ready for use. We also note that all of the passwords are simple dictionary words like effort, points, double, pencil, etc. He later uses that knowledge to enter the school computer system and modify his grades to the desired level.

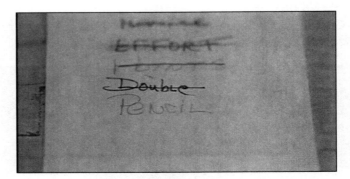

This example from a Hollywood movie is actually based on some real facts. People hate remembering more than two or three passwords, so they try to apply them to all their services and accounts. This is exactly what a responsible administrator must not do. Using simple and standard dictionary words (dog, cat, table), or other personal or institutional names and idioms as your password is a serious security breach. It exposes your system to a possible "dictionary attack".

Dictionary attack is a technique for defeating authentication mechanisms by trying to determine its pass-phrase by searching likely possibilities.

An example of bad password would be *john1975* or *master*.

An example of good password would be *WxIYAURj*.

You can generate passwords using one of the free online sites like `www.freepasswordgenerator.com`.

Removing unnecessary software packages

An important step in securing your Linux server is to determine its primary role. An administrator should know exactly what is installed on his system because otherwise it could be difficult to secure everything available, and overall security will be lower than it should be. You should review the list of packages installed and remove unnecessary packages that do not comply with your security policy. If you do this properly, you will have a lean system that occupies minimal resources and a limited list of packages to update and maintain when security alerts and patches are released. For example, if you do not use FTP, remove it. It is also a good policy not to have any development packages on a production server. Unless you need custom compiled packages, try to build them on a separate machine and deploy them precompiled to all the other production boxes.

Patching

All software has bugs, and those bugs can prevent it from functioning properly. Some of the bugs do not directly affect program functioning, but instead create security holes. These security holes can be (and often are) exploited by malicious attackers. It is therefore crucial to update all of your essential packages either from a distribution repository or by manual installation. CentOS offer updates through YUM.

The Yellowdog Updater, Modified (YUM) is an open source command-line package-management utility for RPM-compatible Linux operating systems.

As a responsible administrator you should evaluate all package updates and decide if you should perform the update or not. It is recommended to have a written security policy and procedure to handle Linux security updates and issues. Assuming we will have Moodle installed on a single production machine with Linux, Apache, MySQL, and PHP (also known as **LAMP**); we should primarily focus on these packages and make sure they are updated accordingly.

Apache configuration

Apache web server is one of the most popular implementations of web server on UNIX-like operating systems. As of February 2010, Apache served over 54 percent of all websites on the Internet. It is a stable and reliable software recommended for both high and small load websites. It is easily configurable and highly flexible because it features modular design which permits to use only parts of the functionality that we really need. This reduces memory footprint and makes server faster to operate and respond. We still must be sure that it is properly configured in terms of basic functionality and security.

Where to start

When attackers want to infiltrate a website they start first by probing for server information. If not properly configured, a web-server can expose sufficient information to the prying eye that can enable the attacker to find a security hole and access private data or services.

All communication between the web browser and web server is performed according to the **Hyper-Text Transfer Protocol (HTTP)**. This protocol is fairly simple. A client sends a request for a resource and the server responds with an appropriate response which can be either a requested resource, or some other response stating an error or asking for additional user input.

Every request or response contains two major parts—**request/response headers** and **request/response body**. The web server can put different information in its response headers. A common example would be something like this:

```
HTTP/1.1 200 OK
Date: Wed, 02 Jun 2010 02:56:36 GMT
Server: Apache/2.2.12 (Unix) mod_ssl/2.2.12 OpenSSL/0.9.7d mod_
wsgi/3.2 Python/2.6.5rc2
Last-Modified: Tue, 01 Jun 2010 07:43:19 GMT
Etag: "22a50e6-4bb8-487f3208173c0"
Accept-Ranges: bytes
Cache-Control: max-age=86400
```

```
Expires: Thu, 03 Jun 2010 02:56:36 GMT
Vary: Accept-Encoding
Content-Encoding: gzip
Content-Length: 5423
Keep-Alive: timeout=5, max=100
Connection: Keep-Alive
Content-Type: text/html
```

The line that is most troublesome is `Server`. This is because the header web-server can choose to expose additional information about the software it uses. By reading this line we know we are dealing with Apache version 2.2.12 with SSL installed using OpenSSL 0.9.7d, mod_wsgi 3.2 and python 2.6.5rc2. All of that is running under UNIX. This is a lot of information to be available for an attacker. Too much! So let us see how we can disable this detailed expose of the server's software.

ServerTokens directive configures the appearance of HTTP Server response header, and as of version 2.0.44 of Apache, it also controls footer content on the error pages.

This directive can have the following values:

- Prod: Display only the product name (Apache)
- Major: Display product name and major version (Apache/2)
- Minor: Display product name and minor version (Apache/2.2)
- Min: Display product name and minimal version (Apache/2.2.12)
- OS: Display product, minimal version, and operating system (Apache/2.2.12 (Unix))
- Full (or not specified): Display product name, minimal version, operating system, and any particular modules executed by web-server (Apache/1.3.41 (Unix) PHP/5.2.12RC4-dev)

All main configurations of Apache web server are located in `/etc/httpd/conf/httpd.conf`. Open a `httpd.conf` in your favorite text editor and add this line:

```
ServerTokens Prod
```

The result of this change is that only the web-server name is displayed. This does not help the attacker much in his preparation for attack since he does not know which version of the software is running, and on what OS it is running on.

There is another thing you should configure in order to minimize exposed information. When we enter an incorrect URL location, the web server usually responds with a message like **Page not found**. However, it can also generate a page footer that exposes similar information as the Server header.

> ## Not Found
>
> The requested URL /stroodle was not found on this server.
>
> ---
>
> *Apache/2.2.15 (Win32) mod_ssl/2.2.15 OpenSSL/0.9.8k Server at localhost Port 80*

It is also advisable to disable the exposure of this information. You can do this by adding this to `httpd.conf`:

```
ServerSignature Off
```

And this is the result:

> ## Not Found
>
> The requested URL /stroodle was not found on this server.

Directory browsing

By default, Apache comes preconfigured to allow directory browsing. This is also considered a security breach as it permits insight into our web application structure and file content. To disable this, we must locate the `DocumentRoot` configuration in `httpd.conf` and find a line that looks like this:

```
Options Indexes FollowSymLinks
```

And change it to:

```
Options -Indexes FollowSymLinks
```

We should repeat this in any directory configuration that is located outside the server DocumentRoot. That way if we try to browse some folder we will get a message like this:

> ## Forbidden
>
> You don't have permission to access /stroodle/ on this server.

Load only a minimal number of modules

Functionality in Apache is added through modules. To reduce the number of potential security holes in your web server, always load minimum number of modules, just the ones that permit your service to operate correctly. Here is an example list of modules:

```
LoadModule auth_basic_module modules/mod_auth_basic.so
LoadModule auth_digest_module modules/mod_auth_digest.so
LoadModule authn_file_module modules/mod_authn_file.so
LoadModule authz_host_module modules/mod_authz_host.so
LoadModule include_module modules/mod_include.so
LoadModule log_config_module modules/mod_log_config.so
LoadModule expires_module modules/mod_expires.so
LoadModule deflate_module modules/mod_deflate.so
LoadModule headers_module modules/mod_headers.so
LoadModule setenvif_module modules/mod_setenvif.so
LoadModule mime_module modules/mod_mime.so
LoadModule negotiation_module modules/mod_negotiation.so
LoadModule dir_module modules/mod_dir.so
LoadModule alias_module modules/mod_alias.so
LoadModule rewrite_module modules/mod_rewrite.so
LoadModule php5_module /usr/lib/php/libphp5.so
```

Install and configure ModSecurity

ModSecurity is a web application firewall that can work either embedded, or as a reverse proxy. It provides protection from a range of attacks against web applications and allows for HTTP traffic monitoring, logging, and real-time analysis. It is quite a complex system, and as such goes beyond the scope of this book. For further information refer to the ModSecurity website: http://www.modsecurity.org/.

MySQL configuration

Database is a crucial element of any LMS. In this way, Moodle is no different than all the other platforms. The recommended database for Moodle is MySQL. Most of the development is done using that RDBMS which makes it therefore less error prone and better tested than the other options. This, of course, does not imply that we can just sit back and enjoy the benefits of the default installation that comes with CentOS. Here is the checklist we should go over that improves our setup of MySQL:

1. **Don't use MyISAM engine**: CentOS 5.4 comes with MySQL 5.0.77. By default, this version uses the MyISAM engine for storing data. MyISAM is good as a storage engine for most of the read-oriented websites, but as soon as we get a lot of writing it tends to break. Apart from security, we also need reliability. Therefore we should switch the default DB engine to the much better InnoDB. To do that, open the MySQL configuration file located in /etc/my.cnf and add these lines in the [mysqld] section:

   ```
   default-character-set=utf8
   default-storage-engine=innodb
   ```

2. **Change the default password of superuser**: The default superuser with complete rights over a database is called root. In the default configuration, that user does not have a password. We must not permit that to happen. We should at least change the password of that user to something more complex, or even better, rename the user root to something else. This will create an additional level of obfuscation if an attacker attempts to obtain the password for the root account by brute force.

3. **Remove the sample database**: MySQL installs a sample database by default called "test". Best practice dictates that we should remove this. Always provide only the minimal necessary level of resources and services that permit your server to operate correctly.

4. Access Moodle database as unprivileged user and grant only minimum of privileges to that account. Please refer back to Chapter 1 for further explanation.

5. **Restrict or disable remote access to the database**: If you host MySQL on the same machine where Moodle is installed then you will never need external access to your database. You can disable the TCP/IP protocol support and all of the communication will be done through UNIX sockets. Add or uncomment this line in /etc/my.cnf.

   ```
   skip-networking
   ```

6. If you use additional web applications or other programs that do not support connections through UNIX Sockets, do not disable TCP/IP. Just force the server to accept connections only from localhost.

   `bind-address=127.0.0.1`

7. **Disable symbolic links**: Add the following option to your configuration file.

   `symbolic-links=0`

8. Make sure you have the latest updates installed for your distribution.

> If you want to have a more recent version of MySQL you can obtain certified builds from MySQL free of charge. You will need the following packages:
>
> MySQL-client-community, MySQL-server-community, and MySQL-shared-community.

9. Have in mind that MySQL does not provide rpm repository so you will have to manually download and install these packages. Visit `http://dev.mysql.com/downloads/mysql/` for more information.

PHP configuration

PHP stands for **PHP: Hypertext Preprocessor**. This kind of idiom is known as a **recursive acronym**. A recursive acronym is an acronym that refers to itself in the expression for which it stands. It is widely used in programming since recursion is one of the common methods used in everyday programming. PHP is an open source, general purpose scripting language widely used for web development. Moodle is completely written in PHP and therefore to run Moodle we need to install and configure PHP. As any other software PHP has potential and real security problems. Because of that we need to be sure that it is configured properly in order to reduce potential security issues.

Installation

To install the PHP that comes with CentOS, execute the following commands from the command prompt:

```
yum install php php-cli php-common php-gd php-mysql php-mbstring php-xml
php-xmlrpc php-tidy
```

This version of PHP is not the latest so we need even more security. Luckily there is the **Suhosin** plugin. Suhosin is an advanced protection system for PHP installations. It was designed to protect servers and users from known and unknown flaws in PHP applications and the PHP core.

To install the Suhosin extension for CentOS 5 execute the following commands:

```
cd /etc/yum.repos.d/
wget http://dev.centos.org/centos/5/CentOS-Testing.repo
yum --enablerepo=c5-testing install php-suhosin
```

With this installation you might have the following issues when running Moodle:

- No further patches will be released for CentOS 5
- No direct route to Moodle 2.0 upgrade. Minimal version of PHP required by Moodle 2 is 5.2.8
- Common Cartridge support will not work since the version of libxml2 that ships with distribution is too old

Your options are to either:

- Wait for the next major release of OS
- Manually compile and install a more recent version of PHP
- Install precompiled certified PHP distribution

Here is the checklist that will improve your PHP security:

1. Disable error displaying in the web browser — display_errors.

   This is an important piece of advice since displaying all errors and notices can show valuable system internals to the potential attacker. This setting should be disabled.

   ```
   display_errors = Off
   ```

2. Disable displaying of startup errors.

   ```
   display_startup_errors=0
   ```

3. Disable exposure of PHP information in server headers.

   ```
   expose_php = 0
   ```

4. Enable error logging.

5. We should always have a log of server activity, therefore every log information counts. Enable this with these statements:

   ```
   log_errors=On
   error_log = '/var/log/php.log'
   ```

6. Features that should be disabled if possible:

   ° `allow_url_fopen`

   ° `allow_url_include`

   ° `magic_quotes_gpc`

   ° `magic_quotes_runtime`

   ° `magic_quotes_sybase`

   ° `enable_dl`

   ° `register_globals`

7. We disable option in `php.ini` by setting the value of the parameter to **Off**. For example:

```
allow_url_fopen = Off
allow_url_include = Off
magic_quotes_gpc = Off
```

> CentOS 5 has PHP version 5.1.6. That is a quite an old version (released in August 2006) with a lot of bugs and security holes that are well known to attackers. The CentOS team will not update PHP until the upcoming release of CentOS 6 which will have PHP 5.3.1 or more recent. If you require a more recent version of PHP you will either have to compile it yourself or install Zend Server Community Edition which is a free, certified version of PHP available for all major operating systems. Visit `http://www.zend.com/products/server-ce/` for more information.

File security permissions

A computer server is a source of many services, resources, and facilities. Some of these are open for public use while others may be protected. The system that permits an authority to specify and control access of individuals to areas and resources in a server is called the **Access Control System (ACS)**. In Linux almost every resource available in the system is defined as a file-system object. Therefore a crucial part of Linux security is file system permission. The following sections describe the several types of ACS available today.

Discretionary Access Control—DAC

This is the basic type of access protection based on the identity of the subjects and/or groups to which they may or may not belong. It is discretionary because a subject with certain permissions is capable of passing that permission on to any other subject. Linux implements DAC using the concept of owner. Every object in the file-system must have an owner and a group specified. Owner controls permissions to access the object. Any other user or group falls into the category of **other**. Filesystems can have files and directories. There are three basic file permissions:

- **Read (r)**: Read access on a file means you can read the content of that file
- **Write (w)**: Write access on a file means you can write into that file
- **Execute (x)**: Execute access on a file means you can run the file

Directory permissions

There are three basic directory permissions:

- **Read (r)**: Read access on a directory means you can read the names of the files and other directories inside.
- **Write (w)**: Write access on a directory means you can create new files or delete/rename existing files regardless of the permissions individual files may have. However, neither of these will work unless you have the execute permission. Without it, write permission is meaningless.
- **Execute (x)**: Execute access on a directory means you can enter into that directory and traverse through the directory tree.

To demonstrate better how permissions apply to a folder, here are several examples:

`drwx------  2 test test   4096 May 25 21:04 group`—User **test** can do everything in group directory.

`dr--------  2 test test   4096 May 30 01:02 group`—User **test** can list the content of the directory.

`dr-x------ 2 test test    6 May 30 01:05 group`—User can do everything except create, delete, or rename files.

`d-wx------ 2 test test    6 May 30 01:05 group`—User can do everything except list the files in the directory. Files can be accessed if name is already known.

`d--x------ 2 test test    6 May 30 01:05 group`—User can do everything except create, rename, and delete files.

Access Control Lists

Files and directories have permission sets for the owner of the file, the group associated with the file, and all other users for the system. However, these permission sets have limitations. For example, different permissions cannot be configured for different users. Thus, Access Control Lists (ACLs) were implemented. So in terms of a file system, in short Access Control Lists are a list of permissions attached to an object. This enables fine-grained settings on both user and operation levels. On Linux (starting from Kernel 2.6) ACL is a standard part of all supported file systems (EXT3, ReiserFS, JFS, XFS, etc.). By default it is not enabled on most distributions.

Mandatory Access Control (MAC)

Mandatory Access Control (MAC) is a security mechanism that restricts the level of control that users (subjects) have over the objects that they create. Unlike in a DAC implementation, where users have full control over their own files, directories, etc., MAC adds additional labels, or categories, to all file system objects. Users and processes must have the appropriate access to these categories before they can interact with these objects. On RedHat-based distributions this system is enforced through SELinux which is one of the MAC implementations on Linux. SELinux is a rather complex subject and as such goes beyond the scope of this book. Our recommendation is to keep it enabled on your server(s).

Adequate location for a Moodle installation

RedHat-based Linux distributions closely follow the File System Hierarchy Standard. This standard contains a set of requirements and guidelines for file and directory placement under UNIX-like operating systems. According to this standard any variable set of data should be placed in the /var directory. This directory is assumed to be on a separate partition (whenever possible) and it is mounted as read/write. Under CentOS, Apache web server has a special directory designated to its needs — /var/www. The default directory for any web file is /var/www/html. Files placed in that directory are located on the **www** root of the web server.

As we already know, Moodle has two major directories. One contains Moodle itself (usually called **Moodle**) while the other has all user and platform data that can change during the course of usage (usually **Moodledata**).

There are numerous options available as to where to install Moodle files. Three such possible options are:

1. Quick and simple installations:

    Moodle is placed in `/var/www/html/moodle`.

    Moodledata is placed in `/var/www/moodledata`.

> A quick way of doing this kind of deploy:
> ```
> mkdir /var/www/moodledata
> cd /tmp/
> wget http://download.moodle.org/download.php/direct/
> stable19/moodle-weekly-19.tgz
> tar -C /var/www/html/ -xzf /tmp/moodle-weekly-19.tgz
> ```

2. Deploying Moodle as distribution package (rpm):

    Moodle is placed in `/usr/share/moodle`.

    Moodledata is placed in `/var/lib/moodle`.

    Apache is configured with an alias to this folder like this:

```
Alias /moodle /usr/share/moodle

<Directory /usr/share/moodle/>
Order Deny,Allow
Allow from all
AllowOverride None
</Directory>
```

3. Custom layout—good for servers that host more than one site:

    All sites are placed in `/sites` directory.

    Moodle is placed in `/sites/moodle1/html/moodle`.

    Moodledata is placed in `/sites/moodle1/moodledata`.

Apache is configured with a virtual host directive like this:

```
<VirtualHost *:80>
ServerName mymoodle.srv.org
DocumentRoot /sites/moodle1/html
<Directory /sites/moodle1/html>
AllowOverride None
Allow from All
</Directory>
</VirtualHost>
```

How to secure Moodle files

Securing Moodle files means to permit only the needed users and groups to access the files in both the `Moodle` and the `moodledata` folder. We will approach this task by using standard DAC methods, and later mention alternatives available with ACL.

DAC

In CentOS, the user under which the Apache process is executed is called **Apache**. That user is a member of the group apache. Therefore, we need to give read-only access to all of the files in the Moodle folder and full read/write access in moodledata. Assuming that we use first option for deploying files, here are the set of commands to set adequate permissions for `moodledata`:

```
/bin/chown -R root:apache /var/www/moodledata/
/bin/chmod -R ug=rwX,o= /var/www/moodledata/
```

The first line sets the owner of the folder (superuser root) and permitted user group (apache). We do this because, as explained earlier, the owner has full rights over anything related to the particular file system object. In case a malicious user manages to break into the system using the web server he will only be able to do limited damage. The web server user is Apache, and since that user is not the owner of either moodle or moodledata, it will not be able to change the ownership of files or modify any other permission. The second line assigns read/write permissions on all files and directories within user and group, and also assigns execute permission to the directories only.

> Keep in mind that these permissions are applied to the objects currently present within the moodledata directory. Anything else in that directory will be created later by the web server which will be the actual owner of all those newly created objects.

Settings for moodle directory:

```
/bin/chown -R root:apache /var/www/html/
/bin/chmod -R u=rwX,g=rX,o= /var/www/html/
```

Rationale is similar to the moodledata directory. The only major difference here is that the user named Apache will have read-only access to both files and folders since there is no need whatsoever for write access.

After creating the configuration file `config.php` for your installation of Moodle make sure it is read-only.

ACL

In case you have installed Moodle on an ACL-enabled file-system, you can enforce even more sophisticated permissions.

Settings for moodledata directory:

```
/bin/chown -R root:root /var/www/moodledata/
/bin/chmod -R u=rwX,go= /var/www/moodledata/
/usr/bin/setfacl -R -m u:apache:rwx /var/www/moodledata/
```

This way we are permitting only the user apache to work with moodledata without adding the group, thus making it a bit more secure.

Settings for moodledata:

```
chown -R root:root /var/www/html/moodle/
chmod -R u=rwX,go= /var/www/html/moodle/
setfacl -R -m u:apache:r /var/www/lms/moodle/
find /var/www/html/moodle/ -type d -execdir setfacl -m u:apache:rx {} \;
```

This basically repeats the settings for moodledata with the exception that user apache can only access files and traverse directory structure.

Summary

We learned some basic facts about securing a Linux-based Moodle server: What web server and database server we need to use, how to install and configure MySQL, PHP, and Apache,.and what hat alternatives are available for MySQL and PHP. Explanation was given about file security system in Linux and the reader will feel more comfortable next time he sees acronyms like DAC, ACL, MAC, and SELinux. Next stop—how to transform your Windows server into an impenetrable fortress!

3
Securing Your
Server—Windows

Somebody or something open to attack or damage is considered vulnerable. A computer system is considered vulnerable if it is susceptible to the operations that try to disrupt, degrade, steal, or destroy information resident on it. As we explained in the first chapter, the weak points of every server intended for hosting Moodle are operating system, web server, PHP, database server, and Moodle itself. In this chapter we will explain how to properly install and configure all of these elements assuming that the operating system is Windows. By properly configuring all crucial elements of a Moodle server, we reduce the possibility of any security breaches and can offer a reliable and stable platform to our users or institutions. If you do not use Windows, then you can skip this chapter. The content is divided into the following topics:

- Securing Windows — the basics
- File security in Windows
- Recommended installation and configuration of PHP under Windows web server
- Recommended installation and configuration of MySQL

Securing Windows—the basics

In this chapter and throughout this book whenever we speak about Windows we speak about Windows 2008 server. The reason we choose to focus on this particular version is that it is the latest version with which most of the new servers will be shipped and which also brings numerous performance and security enhancements particularly related to PHP. Because of this choice, web server and PHP configuration sections are not applicable to the previous versions of Windows OS. The rest can be applied to Windows 2003 provided that you have installed at least Service Pack 2.

Firewall

Windows 2008 ships with an integrated firewall. The firewall is enabled by default and it blocks any incoming connection unless it is the direct response to a previous outgoing request from the computer or unless it is permitted by specific rule created to allow that traffic.

To access the Firewall management console, open **Control Panel** and start the **Windows Firewall** Applet. You will see a dialog similar to the following one:

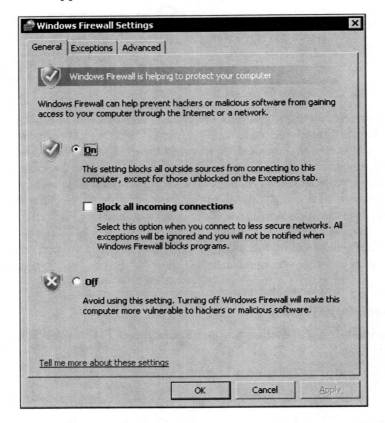

If for whatever reason it is not enabled, enable it making sure that the **Block all incoming connections** option is not checked.

To permit external users to access the web server we need to open HTTP and HTTPS ports. To do that you should click on the **Exceptions** tab and check the following options:

- Core Networking
- Remote desktop
- Secure World Wide Web services (HTTPS)
- World Wide Web services (HTTP)

(Not all options are visible on the screenshot we have provided, but just scroll the list up and you will find them).

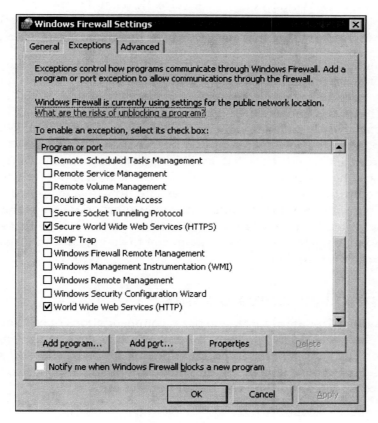

In case you need to fine-tune the firewall settings go to **Control Panel**, choose **Administrative Tools**, and start **Windows Firewall with Advanced Security**. Another way of doing this is to open **Run** dialog and enter this in a command line:

```
%SystemRoot%\system32\WF.msc
```

A quick way of executing programs in Windows is **Run** dialog. You can open it by pressing windows key + R. Enter the executable location and click on **OK**.

Keeping OS updated

Updating Windows is extremely important. It is the most widespread operating system. Due to the large number of people willing to probe for security holes it is one of the most attacked targets on the Internet. Microsoft issues a large number of patches every month for all supported versions of their OS. They are delivered to the customers through the Windows Update service. By default this service is enabled and you should keep it that way. It is essential that you regularly update Windows because that way you are sure that any security or functional issues are resolved.

We need to configure Windows Update to behave according to our needs. Have in mind that you are preparing a machine that will be used as a service provider. Providing a service means you have certain guaranty about its availability. Due to the way Windows is implemented it is often required to restart the OS in order to fully apply a newly installed update. In the default configuration of Windows Update all updates are applied without user intervention, which means that if an update requires the OS to be restarted it will be done automatically. During the process of restarting the OS our service will not be available and if for whatever reason the update did not go well we may even end up with a malfunctioning server. As a responsible administrator you must anticipate appropriate time for applying updates to the system and notify all users about downtime. To have that kind of control we should configure Windows Update not to download and install updates as they appear in the repository.

Configuring Windows update

To set up Windows Update according to our recommendations open **Control Panel** and choose **Windows Update** applet. In the new window, click on the **Change settings** option and configure the **Important updates** option by choosing **Check for updates but let me choose whether to download and install them**. Also uncheck the **Recommended updates** and **Who can install updates** options.

Anti-virus

More than 90 percent of created viruses are for Windows. That makes it extremely vulnerable to this kind of attack. On a desktop machine anti-virus is a must, but on the server things are a bit different.

A server is a dedicated type of machine which, usually, only serves content to outside users. It is extremely rare that outside users can change anything in the server's backend, and even if that is the case it is usually under controlled conditions. The only person who actually works with server content is you — the administrator. Therefore there is no real need to install any anti-virus product. Installing it can even make things worse, especially with a database, since all runtime checking engines verify files on every access/read/write operation.

Imagine now if that file is a big database being scanned every time a new modification is stored. It may have a notable performance impact on the server. We strongly advise against anti-virus on a web server with MySQL database. However, if you still want to install it or must due to your company security policy, make sure you do not configure it to be too aggressive in its checking or set it up to scan only directories which receive content from outside users.

New security model

With Windows Vista/2008, Microsoft introduced a new security model called Mandatory Integrity Control (MIC) which is a version of Mandatory Access Control (MAC). This mechanism is able to selectively restrict the access permissions of certain programs or software components in contexts that are considered to be potentially less trustworthy, compared with other contexts running under the same user account that are more trusted.

There are four **Integrity Levels (IL)** — Low, Medium, High, and System. By default all standard users are assigned Medium IL. This means that no action that affects system components marked with High IL can be executed by such user. That also applies to Administrator. In order to execute a task that affects any core system element, the user needs to elevate his IL to High. When the system detects the need for elevated privileges it will ask the user for confirmation and credentials to confirm and validate IL elevation. This is handled by User Account Control (UAC).

This security model is applied on all running applications within OS but in this case it is relevant only to the administrator since it is essential to know how to obtain administrator privileges in this OS and thus manipulate the configuration process properly.

To elevate command prompt you need to right-click on the command prompt icon in the Start menu and choose the option **Run as administrator**.

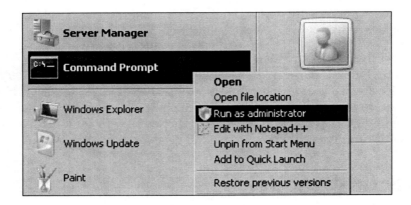

File security permissions

Access Control System in Windows is completely based on Access Control Lists (ACL) and in this aspect it is quite different from Linux. Windows has a list of permissions / actions that can be performed over any object in the operating system and based on the ACL assigned to it OS determines whether to give the access to the user or not. This applies to any resource in the operating system, not just to the element of the file-system.

These are the standard set of file-system permissions available in Windows (simplified list):

- Full control: A user with this permission can do anything
- Modify: Ability to modify file system objects
- Read and Execute: Gives a user ability to traverse through folder(s), list its content, read files, and execute them
- Read: A user can open and read contents of any file
- Write: A user can store the modified files
- List folder content: A user can list content of a specific folder

Every file object can have a DACL (Discretionary Access Control List) that contains different **Access Control Entries (ACE)**. Each of those entries can specify a set of permissions or prohibitions for a particular user or group. Have in mind that the system implicitly denies any kind of access not specified for a particular user.

For example, we have user John and give him read-only permission on file `test.txt`. If he tries to delete that file, the system will inform him that he does not have adequate permissions to perform such operation. In the next section you will see a real-life example of file permissions applicable to Moodle and other software pieces of your server.

Adequate location for Moodle installation

By default the web root folder for IIS 7 is located on base system partition (usually `C:`) in the `inetpub\wwwroot` directory. This is not the place where we should install Moodle. Moodle should be installed in a completely separate directory preferably on non-system partition dedicated only to data storing. In our example, we have a partition Z: which we will use for all non-OS applications. First let us download Moodle. Open the elevated command prompt and execute this:

```
mkdir Z:\temp
bitsadmin /transfer getmoodle /priority HIGH http://download.moodle.
org/download.php/direct/stable19/moodle-weekly-19.zip Z:\temp\moodle-
weekly-19.zip
```

Now create the directory structure and apply appropriate security settings:

```
mkdir Z:\moodledata
icacls Z:\moodledata /Q /T /inheritance:r
icacls Z:\moodledata /Q /T /grant Administrators:(OI)(CI)(F)
icacls Z:\moodledata /Q /T /grant moodle:(OI)(CI)(F)


mkdir Z:\website
icacls Z:\website /Q /T /inheritance:r
icacls Z:\website /Q /T /grant Administrators:(OI)(CI)(F)
icacls Z:\website /Q /T /grant moodle:(OI)(CI)(RX)
```

With the above commands we created `moodledata` directory and assigned full permissions to both Administrators group and Moodle user, which we specially created for running the Moodle website. We also created the parent directory where Moodle files will be placed. Administrators group received full permissions over that directory while user moodle got only read permissions. However, in both cases we configured both directories to automatically apply the same permissions on any newly added file or directory within them.

Extract downloaded file using Compression support in Windows Explorer to `z:\website`. To do this, open Windows Explorer and navigate to `z:\temp`. Right-click on the `moodle-weekly.zip` file and choose the **Extract All** option.

Installing and securing PHP under Internet Information Server

Internet Information Server (IIS) is a default web server shipped with Windows (like Apache is on Linux). In its latest incarnation it brought numerous improvements over the previous versions. One of the biggest criticisms of the previous versions is its monolithic implementation that used too many system resources and did not permit fine-grained configuration of its services. That is no longer the case. Administrator is now able to install and activate only services required by his web application. Another criticism was directed towards less performing implementation of script extensions. This means that PHP could never be as optimized and as fast compared to Apache web server. Because of that, Microsoft implemented FastCGI for IIS 7 and at the same time worked with the PHP community to produce fast and reliable PHP connector. In order to secure our Moodle instance we need to make web server as secure as possible. The way to do that is to install and configure PHP as FastCGI scripting engine.

FastCGI rationale

CGI (Common Gateway Interface) programs are executables launched by the web server for each request in order to process the request and generate dynamic responses that are sent back to the client. CGI has poor performance due to the high cost of starting and shutting down a process for each request (this is more of a problem on Windows than on Linux). FastCGI addresses the performance issues inherent to CGI by providing a mechanism to reuse a single process over and over again for many requests.

To learn more about FastCGI for IIS visit http://www.iis.net/download/FastCGI.

Using FastCGI to run PHP offers complete isolation of the scripting engine and makes it possible to run different versions of PHP in separate websites. Furthermore it is unnecessary to add PHP directory into system PATH, making OS as clean as possible. We will cover the manual process of installing and configuring PHP because every administrator should really understand what happens behind the scenes and be able to easily adapt to any particular circumstances.

Preparing IIS

Before doing anything we need to be sure that IIS is properly set up. Here are the steps you should perform to make sure everything is as it should be:

- Make sure you have installed support for CGI (which includes FastCGI as well). Open the **Server Manager** applet and look into the **WEB Server Role** pane.

> To open server manager go to **Control Panel/Administrative Tools** and start **Server Manager** snap-in or from command line execute this:
>
> `start %SystemRoot%\system32\CompMgmtLauncher.exe`

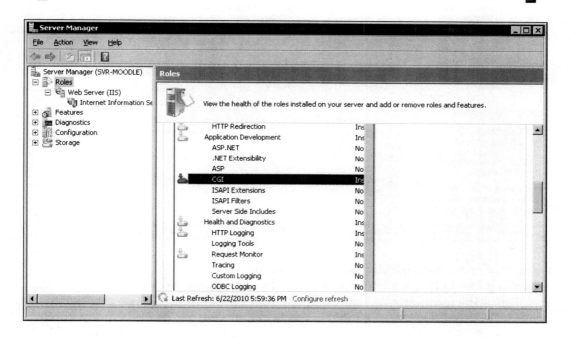

- Install the FastCGI update located at `http://support.microsoft.com/?kbid=980363`. It fixes various problems and improves stability.
- Install Administration pack 1.0. It can be downloaded from this location: `http://www.iis.net/download/AdministrationPack`. With this add-on you get the option to properly configure any FastCGI extension.

Getting the right version of PHP

In order to fully use the capabilities of new FastCGI you should download and install non-thread-safe version of PHP.

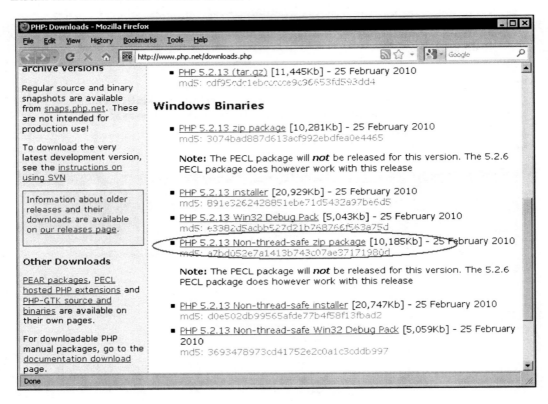

Extract the contents of the ZIP file in a new empty directory. We recommend something like c:\php5. Locate the file php.ini-recommended and rename it to php. ini. This is the recommended starting point for PHP configuration on production servers. On Windows machines PHP expects to find php.ini in the Windows main directory which is usually called Windows. We do not recommend using this kind of deployment. It is highly recommended to have everything related to the particular version of PHP in one and only one main directory (c:\php5 in our example).

Configuring php.ini

Open your newly created `php.ini` in any text editor and start applying the following modifications:

- Locate the line with `expose_php` directive and make sure it looks like this:

```
expose_php = Off
```

- Locate the commented line with `error_log` directive and change it to look like this:

```
error_log ="c:/php5/err.log"
```

Make sure to remove `;` at the beginning of the line so that the directive will have actual effect.

- Locate the `fastcgi.impersonate` directive and uncomment it so that it looks like this:

```
fastcgi.impersonate = 1;
```

- Set `extension_dir` directive to point to <PHP dir>/ext which in our case would be:

```
extension_dir = "c:/php5/ext"
```

- Locate the Windows extensions section in `php.ini` and uncomment (remove `;` from the beginning of every line you want to enable) following lines:

```
extension=php_curl.dll
extension=php_gd2.dll
extension=php_mbstring.dll
extension=php_mysqli.dll
extension=php_openssl.dll
extension=php_xmlrpc.dll
extension=php_xsl.dll
extension=php_zip.dll
```

- Configure time zone: It is highly recommended to configure timezone explicitly in php to ensure proper date and time handling. To do that locate the line with `date.timezone` option and configure it to look like this `date.timezone=<TZ from Olson database>`. For example:

```
date.timezone = America/Detroit
```

To see the list of available time zones visit the PHP documentation page `http://php.net/manual/en/timezones.php`.

Adding PHP to the IIS

Every scripting engine executed inside IIS is assigned to an application pool. Application pool in IIS is an isolated amount of system resources used to run specified executables. To increase security of Moodle and PHP we should do the following:

1. Whenever possible use one website per web application: This is rather an obvious statement. If we have a particular web application and make it exclusive for that website, in case of illegal access the perpetrator will be able to damage only one service which is important especially in a shared hosting environment.

2. Website should have its root folder on a separate non-system partition: With this we isolate the file systems between websites making it impossible to damage one website from another.

3. Website should have separate application pool: By separating scripting engines in various pools we can easily isolate executions between websites and further improve the stability of the execution.

4. An application pool should be using a separate account for executing its processes: By applying a separate account for executing pool processes we give explicit access only to the resources needed and used by a particular web application, again minimizing potential damage and increasing security.

Creating Application pool

Every scripting engine executed inside IIS is assigned to an application pool. An application pool in IIS is an isolated amount of system resources used to run specified executables. They can be created through IIS Manager snap-in. You can start it by going to the **Control Panel | Administrative Tools | Internet Information Services (IIS) Manager**. Click on **Application pools** and choose **Add application pool** on the right side of the manager pane.

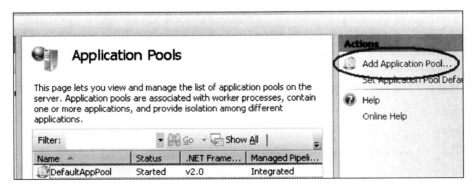

In the new dialog, enter new Application pool name, choose **No Managed Code** in
.NET framework version: option, and leave all the other options as they are.

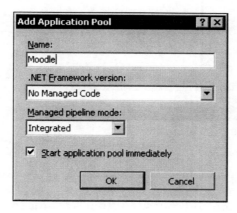

Create a new user that will be used to access Moodle files both by web server and
PHP. To do that, open **Control Panel | Administrative Tools** and choose **Server
Manager**. In **Server Manager** expand **Configuration | Local Users and Groups**
and click on **Users**. Right-click with the mouse in the right pane and choose
option — **New user**.

Go back to the IIS Manager and open the **Application Pools** section. Choose **Moodle Application Pool** and click on the **Advanced Settings…** action located on the right side of the panel.

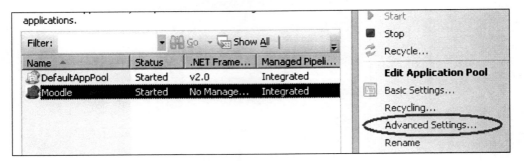

Click on the **Identity option** and choose **Custom Account** and then click on the set button. Enter Moodle for username and the password that you configured during the creation of Moodle account.

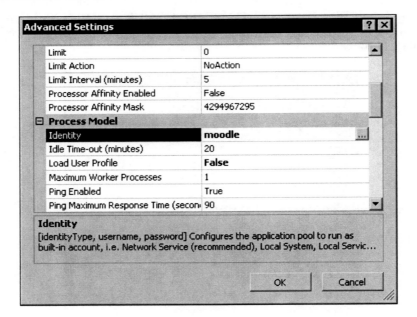

Create new website

Open IIS Manager snap-in and go into the **Sites** section. On the right side of the panel click on the **Add Website** option.

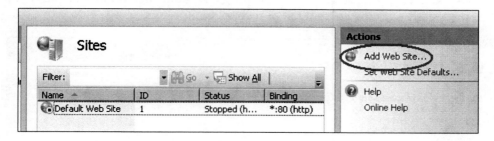

Type the name of your new website (**Moodle**), choose the application pool we just created, specify the physical location of your site (directory where you plan on placing Moodle), and configure the website to use user account Moodle for accessing site resources (**Connect as button**). Once you have finished entering that entire information click **OK**.

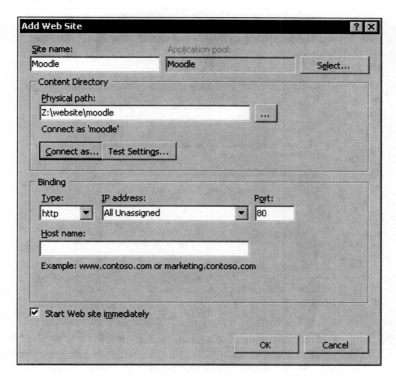

Adding PHP mapping

After all these steps we can finally add PHP support for our newly created website. In IIS Manager click on the **Sites** section and enter into **Moodle** website. Among various options you will see **Handler Mappings**. Double-click on that one and you will be presented with the current list of resource mappings.

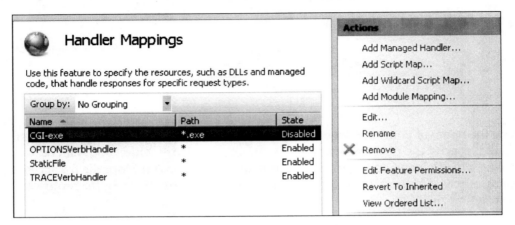

Click on the **Add Module Mapping** option and configure PHP handler as it is presented in the following screenshot:

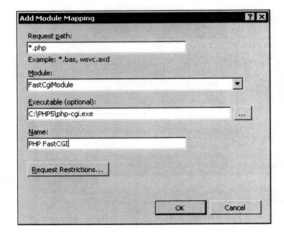

Now just one more step is needed to finish PHP configuration under IIS. We need to specify two environment variables for our FastCGI executable so that it can work properly. To add these variables, once again we go to the IIS Manager and click on the main server home. In there we will see the FastCGI settings icon (this icon is visible only if you installed the IIS Administration pack). We will see all FastCGI handlers configured on our server. In this case we have just one item, php-cgi.exe. Double-click on that item and you will be presented with **Edit FastCGI Application** dialog. The part interesting to us is **EnvironmentVariables**. We need to add two items in this list. First is the **PHPRC** variable. When specified this variable is used by PHP to determine the location of php.ini that should be used during execution. As mentioned before, on Windows by default PHP uses php.ini in Windows system directory. We want it to use the one located in c:\php5. See the following screenshot:

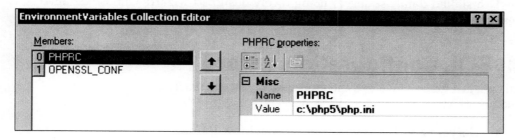

Another variable we need to add is **OPENSSL_CONF**. This one is important because it points to the location of openssl.cnf needed by PHP extension OpenSSL. Without that the variable extension will not work and therefore any part of Moodle that depends on that functionality will also not work. OpenSSL configuration file that ships with standard PHP is always located in <PHP directory>\extras\openssl\ openssl.cnf.

We can now move on to the securing procedure for MySQL server.

Securing MySQL

MySQL as it is installed by default on Windows is neither well configured nor particularly secure. Securing the database is important because if somehow an attacker manages to get access to the underlying data through Moodle, student and institution information may be in danger. Information can be illegally copied or even destroyed which is definitely something we would like to avoid. In the following section we will show a step by step procedure for correctly installing and configuring MySQL server.

Check which version of Windows 2008 you are using (32-bit or 64-bit) and download the appropriate build of MySQL to fully use the resources offered by underlying architecture. To check the version go to Control Panel and open System Applet. We will use MySQL 5.1.47 64-bit. Download your version from this location http://dev.mysql.com/ downloads/mysql/.

Start the installation and choose custom setup. On the next screen configure the location for database files. It is always a better idea to place the database folder on a separate partition thus separating system files from application files. In our case we have a separate partition tied to letter Z and we will place it in a directory called `mysqldata`.

After copying the files, the installer will offer us an option of configuring the newly installed database server using nicely designed wizard. Choose detailed configuration and click on **Next**.

MySQL configuration wizard

This wizard has seven steps through which you can easily configure your instance of MySQL:

- **Server type**: Choose the **Server Machine** option.

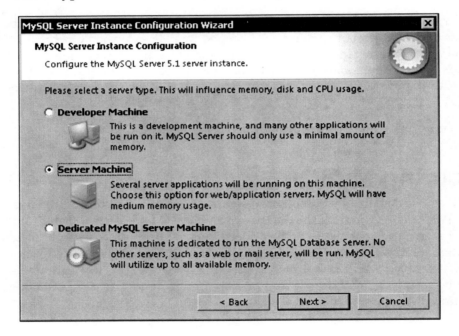

- **Database usage**: Choose **Transactional Database only**.

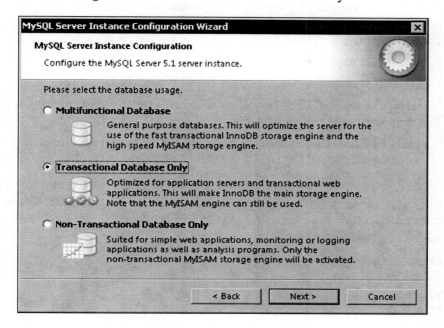

- **Innodb tablespace setting**: Choose the same folder where you decided to place the databases (z:\mysqldata).

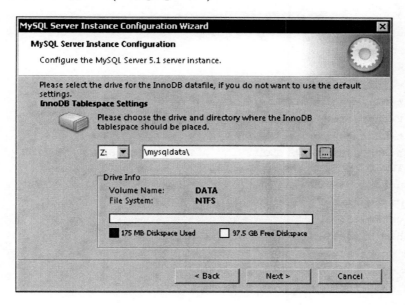

- **Number of concurrent connection**: Choose the **Decision support** option (however, if you plan on serving a high number of concurrent users then choose **Online transaction Processing**).

- **Networking options**: Uncheck **Enable TCP/IP Networking** and check **Enable Strict mode**.

- **Default Character Set**: Choose **Best support for Multilingualism**.

- **Windows options**: Check **Install as Windows service** and uncheck **Include Bin directory in Windows PATH**.

- **Security options**: Check **Modify Security Settings** and specify new password for user root.

After finishing, wizard configuration file my.ini is generated and stored together with MySQL binaries. For example, if you have decided to store the MySQL in directory Z:\mysql, then the configuration file will be stored in the same location. In our case mysql.ini looks like this:

```
[client]
pipe
socket=mysql

[mysql]
default-character-set=utf8

[mysqld]
skip-networking
enable-named-pipe
socket=mysql
basedir="C:/Program Files/MySQL/MySQL Server 5.1/"
datadir="Z:/mysqldata/Data/"
default-character-set=utf8
default-storage-engine=INNODB
sql-mode="STRICT_TRANS_TABLES,NO_AUTO_CREATE_USER,NO_ENGINE_
SUBSTITUTION"
max_connections=100
query_cache_size=0
table_cache=256
tmp_table_size=154M
thread_cache_size=8
innodb_data_home_dir="Z:/mysqldata/"
innodb_additional_mem_pool_size=21M
innodb_flush_log_at_trx_commit=1
```

```
innodb_log_buffer_size=10M
innodb_buffer_pool_size=973M
innodb_log_file_size=487M
innodb_thread_concurrency=8
```

Configure MySQL service to run under low/privileged user

The next step in securing MySQL is to run it using a non-system user account. The default user used to run Windows Services is LocalService which has high execution privileges. We should replace it with a separate user and apply appropriate file permissions on MySQL binary and data files.

Create a mysql account

Create a new user called mysql. To do that, open **Control Panel/Administrative Tools** and choose **Server Manager**. In **Server Manager** expand **Configuration/Local Users and Groups** and click on **Users**. Right-click with the mouse in the right pane and choose option — **New user**.

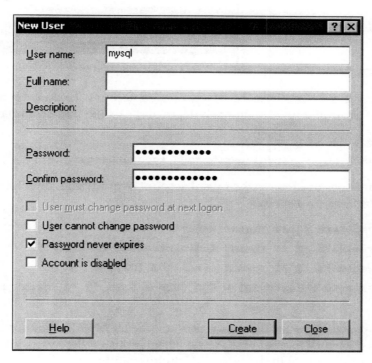

The next step is to add permission to the account mysql to create processes as services. For this you need to open the **Local Security Policy** editor. You will find it in the **Control Panel/Administrative Tool** section. On the right side of the window navigate to **Security Settings/Local Policies/User Rights Assignment** and find the policy on the right side of the screen called **Log on as service**. Double-click on that option and add user mysql to the list of permitted users accounts.

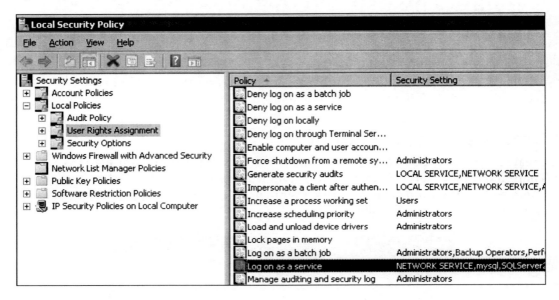

Configure MySQL service to use the newly created account. To do it open the command line prompt with elevated privileges and execute these commands:

```
net stop MySQL
sc config MySQL obj= .\mysql password= <accountpass>
```

Add appropriate permissions to the mysql account over MySQL directories and files. In the command line execute this:

```
icacls Z:\mysqldata /Q /T /inheritance:r
icacls Z:\mysqldata /Q /T /grant Administrators:(OI)(CI)(F)
icacls Z:\mysqldata /Q /T /grant mysql:(OI)(CI)(F)
icacls "C:\Program Files\MySQL\MySQL Server 5.1" /Q /T /grant mysql:(OI)(CI)(RX)
```

This will add permissions for the mysql user to execute MySQL binaries in the Program Files directory and set read/write permissions on the mysqldata directory while retaining full control to the users in Administrators group.

Now start MySQL again by executing this command:

```
net start MySQL
```

Summary

We learned some basic facts on how to properly install and configure basic Windows services, PHP, MySQL, and Moodle in a secure manner. In the next chapter we will talk about logon procedure in Moodle and how to make it as secure as possible.

4
Authentication

Every educational institution offers its services to individuals willing to improve their knowledge in a particular area of study and obtain an appropriate degree. Only enlisted and subscribed participants can visit the lectures and other activities. The same can be applied to Moodle. We want to make sure that the only people using the platform are the ones who should be using it in the first place. Therefore in this chapter we will cover the following topics:

- Basics of authentication
- Common authentication attacks and prevention methods
- Authentication types in Moodle and security tips

Basics of authentication

Authentication is the process of confirming that something or someone is really who they claim to be. The ways in which someone may be authenticated fall into three categories, based on what are known as the factors of authentication:

- Knowledge (something you know): password, PIN code, etc.
- Ownership (something you have): security token, phone, etc.
- Inherence (something you are): fingerprint, signature, various biometric identifiers

Following the path of most computer systems, Moodle offers basic authentication based on a knowledge factor. This means that in order to operate in Moodle any person must have a user account.

A user account consists of a username, password, and other personal information. Both username and password are used to authenticate a person who wishes to access the platform. Based on the outcome of an authentication, a user will be given or declined access to the platform. The authentication is performed (usually) by comparing provided data from the person trying to access the platform with the data located in the Authoritative Data Source (of user identity). Moodle supports 13 different types of authentication and this actually means that it has support for consulting 13 different types of Authoritative Data Sources.

 An Authoritative Data Source is a recognized or official data production source with a designated mission statement or source/product to publish reliable and accurate data for subsequent use by users or by other computer programs.

Logon procedure

Logon in Moodle is implemented using a HTML form that submits supplied data over HTTP or HTTPS to the server where it is being processed.

 Hypertext Transfer Protocol (HTTP) is a networking protocol used for transferring and rendering content on the World Wide Web. **HTTP Secure (HTTPS)** is a combination of a HTTP protocol and SSL/TLS (Security Socket Layer/ Transport Layer Security) protocol that offers encrypted and thus secures communication and identification between two computers on the Internet. HTTPS connections are often used for payments transactions and other sensitive information's transfer.

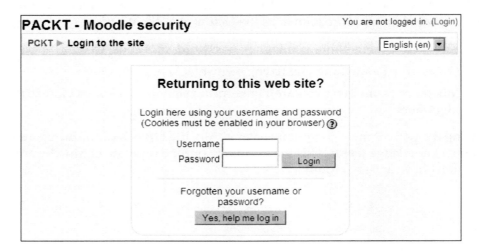

The user enters his assigned credentials into the supplied fields on the login form and presses **Login**. That sends data to Moodle for processing.

Common authentication attacks

Any type of security attack is directed toward potential weak spots in the system that is under attack. The most common weaknesses related to the authentication and ways of protecting from them are as follows:

Weak passwords

A password that is easily guessed and does not provide an effective defense against unauthorized access to a resource is considered weak. Such passwords are usually:

- Short
- Set to dictionary word or name
- Set to be the same as username
- Set to some predefined value

When we have a platform with weak passwords it can be attacked using brute force login technique (also known as dictionary attack).

Dictionary attack is a technique for defeating authentication mechanism by trying to determine its pass-phrase by searching likely possibilities. In practice this means that a bot (automated script) constantly tries to log on by sending various usernames and passwords from a predefined list of words (usually a dictionary list of words—hence the name dictionary attack).

Enforcing a good password policy

In order to prevent this attack, make sure you have enabled the password policy. Visit **Administration | Security | Site policies** and locate the **Password Policy** checkbox. You should arrive at the following screenshot:

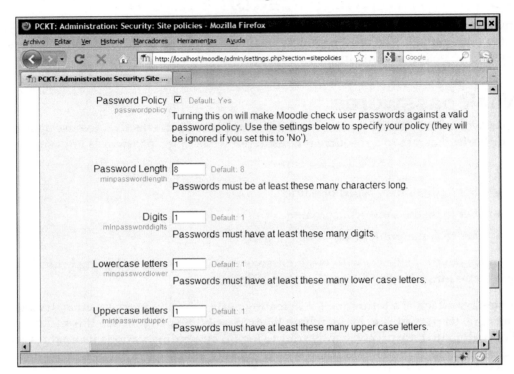

 Password policy is enabled by default starting from Moodle 1.9.7. This applies to both new installs and upgrades.

Protecting user logon

By default, Moodle is configured to use unencrypted HTTP as the main communication protocol between client and server. This is fine for general usage of the platform but it also exposes credential information to the potential eavesdropper who can intercept and read it. This is a common case known as man-in-the-middle attack. The perpetrator makes a separate connection with the client (user's computer) and server (Moodle), forcing all communication to go over his connection. That permits him to look at the entire communication and even inject his own version of messages and responses.

Closing the security breach

We need to make sure that credential transmission is performed using secure HTTP (HTTPS) because that prevents (or makes it really hard) for anybody to hook into a protected conversation. Here are the steps:

Firstly, you should install and configure a valid SSL (Secure Sockets Layer) certificate on your web-server. It is important to do this properly before doing anything else in Moodle; otherwise you might block yourself from accessing the platform. The procedure for installing an SSL certificate is beyond the scope of this book since it involves too many different factors that depend on your server configuration, OS type, and the way you manage it. Please refer to the manual for your particular web server and/or particular procedure of your hosting provider.

> Valid SSL certificates can be obtained only from certified root authorities — companies with a license for issuing certificates. VeriSign, Thawte, and Comodo are one of the several certificate providers. You need to specify which web server you are using since some of them prefer particular formats.

Secondly, you should activate HTTPS log-in in your Moodle. You can do that by going to **Administration | Security | HTTP security** page and checking **Use HTTPS for logins**.

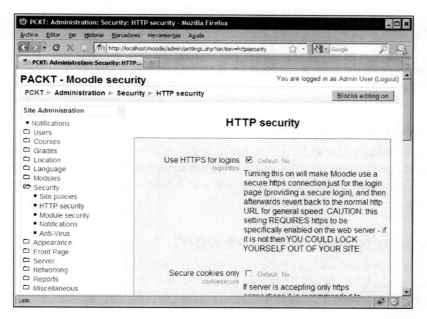

If everything is configured properly you should see a login page that shows a valid certificate box (see following screenshot) in your browser. This means that a certificate is issued by a valid root authority and that communication between your browser and Moodle is secure which is what we wanted to accomplish in the first place.

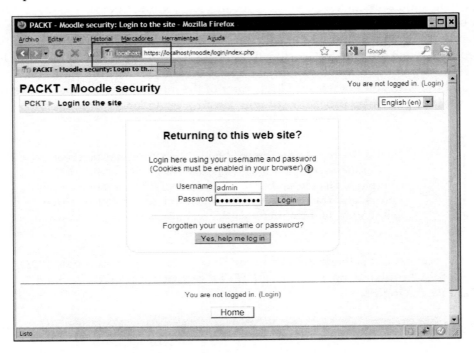

Every time a user tries to login in Moodle they will be redirected to the secure version of the login page which effectively prevents the interception of user credentials.

Password change

By default, all newly created users in Moodle (excluding admin) are assigned the **Authenticated user** role. The authenticated user role by default has permission to change their own password. This feature can be utilized by accessing user profile page.

Recover a forgotten password

Forgetting a username and/or password is a common situation in which many users find themselves. Moodle offers a procedure for getting a username and resetting the password.

The user will be presented with a form where he can enter his username or his e-mail. If the username or email exists in the database, a mail with a reset link will be sent to that user. By clicking on that link, the user is offered a chance to enter a new password.

If not configured properly, this feature can be used for determining valid user emails or user-names. See the following screenshot:

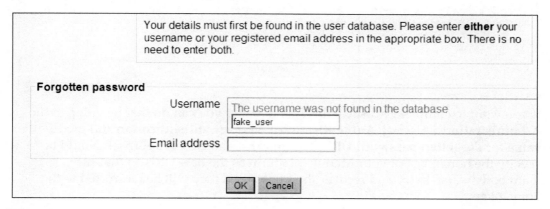

An attacker would be able to tailor a script that could probe for usernames and, based on the response, can determine valid users.

Preventing a potential security risk

To protect from this potential flaw we need to disable error information from being displayed to the user. Go to the **Administration | Security | Site policies** page and make sure the **Protect usernames** option is activated.

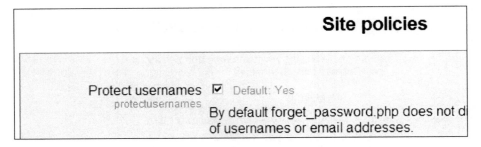

After this change, Moodle displays a different message upon submitting username or mail.

> If you supplied a correct username or email address then an email should have been sent to you.
>
> It contains easy instructions to confirm and complete this password change. If you continue to have difficulty, please contact the site administrator.
>
> Continue

If you want to completely disable this functionality you can do that by going to the **Administration | Users | Authentication | Manage authentication** and modify the value for **Forgotten password URL**. The quickest and easiest approach would be to specify the homepage of your Moodle platform as the new URL. In that case, if anybody wants to try and recover their password they will be redirected to the home page.

 Disabling password recovery may generate an important impact on you as an administrator since all such requests would have to be handled manually.

Securing user profile fields

In Moodle, every user account has a profile. A profile is a set of information describing the user in more detail with information such as their address, ZIP code, telephone number, etc. Almost every authentication plugin has support for handling user profile fields. By default, in all cases a profile is open for user editing. Such configuration is correct when Moodle itself is the **Authoritative Data Source (ADS)** of user information. However, when we authenticate the user against external source, the situation is different. In such cases it is always better to lock profile fields or at least enable them only if they are empty. That way we maintain stable and predictable user information across all our systems. Only two plugins use Moodle as ADS and these are **Manual accounts** and **Email-based-self-registration**. The rest of the plugins synchronize against external sources.

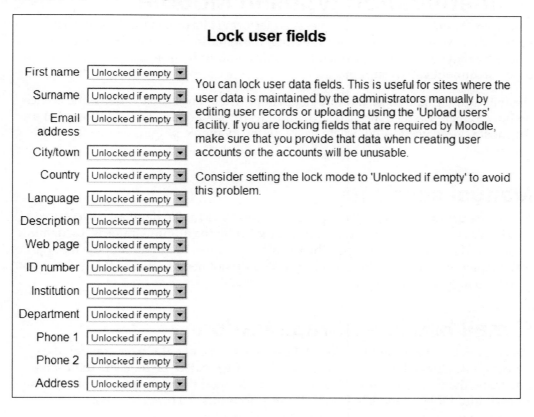

User model in Moodle

Every user account in Moodle has four unique characteristics: username, password, e-mail, and authentication type. The username and e-mail must be unique on the system level and that prevents ambiguities in the platform. The authentication type determines which plugin will take care of credential validation. Bear in mind that Moodle can have more than one authentication plugin active. That is quite a common scenario in various installations. For example, administrative accounts are handled by the **Manual accounts** plugin while students and teachers can be handled by the **LDAP** plugin.

Authentication types in Moodle

One of the better features of Moodle as a platform is its diversity. Educational institutions often have a separate system(s) for handling students' information. Knowing that such a need exists, the Moodle community gradually added various types of authentication support.

We will now explain these in more detail and, where applicable, offer some advice on how to increase their security. The plugins presented here are just those that are the most widely used. A complete list of all the available plugins can be found in *Appendix A*.

Manual accounts

This is the default authentication plugin. It uses the Moodle database as a source of valid user credentials. Any user account created by the administrator is, by default, set to the Manual accounts type. The security measures mentioned in the first part of this chapter are adequate for this plugin. You do not need to do anything else if you plan on using just this plugin.

E-mail based self-registration

This plugin also uses the Moodle database as a source of valid user credentials. What is different is the way in which accounts are created. Here, users themselves can create their own account. Validation is performed through e-mail. This opens a possibility for spammers to create dummy accounts. To prevent robots and unwanted users to start polluting the site we have two options:

Specifying allowed or denied e-mail domains

In case all our users have e-mails in several predefined domains, then we can specify them in the authentication configuration and block any other unwanted e-mail account. This is an excellent way of preventing unwanted users to create an account in our Moodle. For example, if we notice that in last few days we had several hundred accounts created and all were using e-mails with domain `evilhackers.net`, then we can prevent them just by adding that domain to the **Denied email domains**. Visit the **Administration | Users | Authentication | Manage authentication** page and modify the setting according to your particular needs.

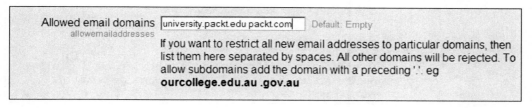

If you want to enforce mail domains restriction in case of changing existing user e-mail addresses, you need to check the appropriate option on the same page.

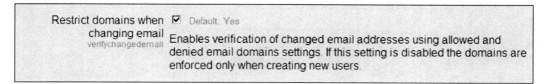

Captcha

Captcha (Completely Automated Public Turing test to tell Computers and Humans Apart) is a challenge-response test used in logon protection to ensure that a response is generated by a human and not by a computer. It is usually implemented in the form of images with drastically distorted letters which are impossible to be deciphered by a computer.

A major problem any site with self-registering capability has is related to automated scripts (bots) that create a bulk of fake accounts usually used for generating spam. This problem is solved by Captcha.

Moodle supports the Google reCaptcha service. Google reCaptcha is a free Captcha service used to protect various online systems against automated logon. It does so by providing a user with a particular image with a couple of words that cannot be analyzed by a computer but are readable to a human. By providing a valid sentence, the user is validated as a human and thus permitted to enter.

You should open a Google account and register for reCaptcha. For this you should visit `http://www.google.com/recaptcha` to register and generate API keys for your platform. The registration procedure is quite straightforward. Just follow the onscreen instructions provided by Google. After you obtain the keys place them on the "Manage Authentication" page. To open that page visit **Administration | Users | Authentication | Manage authentication**.

ReCAPTCHA public key [6LcuQLsSAAAAAKiodylZF9LGurN] Default: Empty
recaptchapublickey
String of characters used to display the reCAPTCHA element in the signup form. Generated by http://recaptcha.net

ReCAPTCHA private key [6LcuQLsSAAAAAOxB6cq_RT5FC] Default: Empty
recaptchaprivatekey
String of characters used to communicate between your Moodle server and the recaptcha.net server. Obtain one for this site by visiting http://recaptcha.net

When the user tries to apply for a new account he will be presented with something like this:

Email address*
Email (again)*
First name*
Surname*
City/town*
Country* Select a country
reCAPTCHA

thick twitted

Enter the words above
Get another CAPTCHA
Get an audio CAPTCHA

Session hijacking

Session hijacking is the exploitation of a valid computer session, sometimes also called a session key to gain unauthorized access to information or services in a computer system. This basically means stealing the magic logon hash from the session cookie.

The most common techniques used for hijacking user session are as follows:

- **Session sniffing**: Communication between client and server is being monitored by a third party. During this interaction the third party can pick up session ID and then use it to directly access server without the need to log in.

- **Cross-site script attack**: Also known as XSS. It involves usage of malicious JavaScript that will be executed inside the client's browser. A common way of deploying this is by sending an e-mail with a specially crafted URL that will transfer sessionID to the hacker.

We have several options offered by Moodle in treating this exploit. On the HTTP security page these options are available:

- **Only http cookies**: This is a new feature available as of PHP 5.2. This means that cookie information is being transferred only through HTTP requests without any access given to the scripting languages. If you use the latest version of PHP and do not have to support legacy web browsers this option is highly recommended.

- **Regenerate session during login**: Creates new session for every login. This is highly recommended for security reasons. It can bring some problems with shared sessions and with some authentication plugins. In general, it works well with manual accounts and self-enrolled accounts. It can also exhibit issues with the users that often change IP (switching from one wireless network to another).

Only http cookies cookiehttponly	☑ Default: No Enables new PHP 5.2.0 feature - browsers are instructed to send cookie with real http requests only, cookies should not be accessible by scripting languages. This is not supported in all browsers and it may not be fully compatible with current code. It helps to prevent some types of XSS attacks.
Regenerate session id during login regenloginsession	☑ Default: Yes Regeneration of the session id during each login request is highly recommended for security reasons. This setting might not be compatible with some authentication plugins.

No login

This plugin is used to disable a particular user account. To do that, go to **Administration | Users | Accounts | Browse list of users** and locate the user you wish to prevent from logging in and click on the **Edit** link.

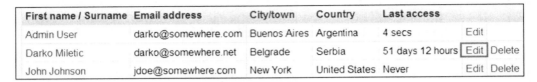

First name / Surname	Email address	City/town	Country	Last access		
Admin User	darko@somewhere.com	Buenos Aires	Argentina	4 secs	Edit	
Darko Miletic	darko@somewhere.net	Belgrade	Serbia	51 days 12 hours	Edit	Delete
John Johnson	jdoe@somewhere.com	New York	United States	Never	Edit	Delete

After that, click on the **Show Advanced** button and modify the **Choose an authentication method** field.

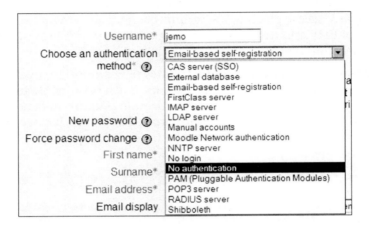

Summary

In this chapter we learned a lot about the Moodle user model. Major security holes in the logon process were covered, along with ways of closing them. You learned about session hijacking, dictionary attack, and ways of fighting against them. We mentioned the most commonly used types of authentication. A clear and exact procedure of configuring and securing those plugins was presented. The final outcome of all this is a much more secure logon/authentication procedure.

There is still a long road ahead of us. We protected the entrance door to your fortress but now we need to focus on internal security. Next stop—Roles and Permissions.

5
Roles and Permissions

Every complex system offers various usage patterns based on user needs and obligations. Based on such use cases we can identify specific roles. Moodle is no different in this respect. For example, we know for sure that we must have a person dedicated to maintaining the platform, monitoring, and fixing any issues that may arise at a time—that person should have the role of a general manager or in Moodle terminology, an administrator. Another example would be a user that is a course participant. His principal interest is to browse through all available learning materials and participate in any tasks set for him—this would be learner or student. Each and every role has a set of things that are permitted or prohibited. By assigning users to one of the predefined or custom roles we are defining the spectrum of the options and actions available to them at every location within LMS. It is paramount for every administrator to fully understand access rights as they are implemented. Therefore, in this chapter we will focus on access rights to resources and functions within Moodle starting with:

- Roles and capabilities
- Standard roles
- Customizing roles
- Best security practices with roles

Roles and capabilities

The Moodle access rights system is based around the concepts of contexts, capabilities, permissions, and roles. Let us first define these terms in the context of Moodle.

Capability

A capability is a system defined feature or action. For example, view course would be one capability. All capabilities are defined either by Moodle core or by third-party module(s).

Context

Context is an abstraction representing part of Moodle. We have six predefined contexts and they are arranged in a hierarchical fashion with permissions inherited from higher to lower contexts. Here is the list of existing contexts presented in order of importance from higher to lower:

- **System**: This context represents the entire Moodle. Any role assigned at this level applies globally on the entire system. For example, if we assign the teacher role to a user he will have that role in every course and would be able to manage them as if enrolled in every one of them.

- **User**: This context for a specific user. It context can be used to assign partial or complete management rights on the user related and generated content outside of the course (profile, blog, messages, etc.). Usually, it is used for giving partial or full access of subject's data to HR staff or relatives/parents.

- **Course category**: The courses always belong to some category, so this context applies to anything within that category or subcategory.

- **Course**: Context for a specific course.

- **Activity**: This context describes particular activity within a course.

- **Block**: This context applies to a particular type of block.

Permissions

Permission defines whether capability is enabled or not. Each capability can be given permission on a particular context. There are four permissions defined:

- **Not set**: If a capability has this setting in a particular context it behaves exactly same as the Prevent permission by default following a rule "prohibit everything that is not explicitly allowed". However, if there is another role in the lower context with a different value then it will override this setting.

- **Allow**: Enables capability.

- **Prevent**: Disables capability in a context for a specific user.

- **Prohibit**: This is effectively the same as **Prevent** but it also prohibits overriding that same capability in lower level contexts.

Role

A Role answers to a question: what can the user do? and is also a predefined list of permissions applied to all capabilities within the system. With Role we can easily separate what one group of users can and cannot do in the specific part of the platform. It is important to say that any user can and usually will have more than one role applied on the same context. Moodle poses no limits in that area, but we still should be conservative in the way we assign and use roles.

How it all fits together

Whenever a user wants to perform a specific action in some context, Moodle checks his permission level for it. This is done by reviewing all permissions from all roles that are assigned to that user at that particular context. The result of that review produces computed permission as a sum of enabled, disabled, or not set values taking into account context precedence.

For example, a user logs into Moodle and wishes to enter into a course. Upon logon, every user is assigned the **Authenticated** user role (this is the default and recommended setting for most use cases but it can be modified). Whether a user can see a course or not is determined by a state of course_view capability for that user within a role he has in that course context. Moodle gets all roles for that user starting from the system level down to the course level. It can be presented with the following table:

User	Context	Role	Capability	Permission
Student1	System	Authenticated user	course_view	not set
	User			
	Course category			
	Course 1	Student	course_view	allowed

As you can see a user has no role whatsoever for some contexts which is normal in Moodle. We are showing them just for the sake of completeness.

In this simple case we have two instances of the course_view capability. One is **not set** while the other is set to **allowed**. The basic formula for calculating resulting permission can be described like this:

Start from the context of the resource we want to access, get user role(s) (if any) for it, and get permission value(s) for specific capability. If a user has more than one role defined in that context, permission values are summed in the resulting value.

If any of the permissions has the value "prohibit" it finishes the check and denies access to the user, otherwise save current computed permission value and go to the parent context. If there is a parent context, repeat the process. Otherwise, return the computed permission. If the final permission value is bigger than or equal to 1, then the user is granted access.

Standard Moodle roles

Moodle has seven predefined roles. They usually cover most of the needs that common educational institutions might have. All of them are created with particular usage patterns in mind. Even if they do not completely fit your needs they are a good starting point for customizations. Because of that, it is important to understand them before using or modifying the role. The list of roles is as follows:

- **Administrator**: It is a role with all permissions enabled by default, and can access everything.

- **Course creator**: It is a role primarily used for instructors who manage and create their own courses. A user with this role automatically gets the role of the Teacher in the course he creates.

- **Teacher**: A user with this role can do anything within the course including assigning grades to the students, seeing submitted assignments, and creating forum topics.

- **Non-editing teacher**: It can grade students but cannot alter course content and/or structure.

- **Student**: A standard role for an educational content consumer. Usually, it has fewer privileges, for example, he can see his grades, forum messages, and his submitted assignments.

- **Guest**: This is a role with minimal privileges used for temporary access to some part of the Moodle. The Moodle administrator can disable guest access if needed.

- **Authenticated user**: This is the role assigned by default to any logged-in user and covers any tasks that a common user can perform outside a course.

Customizing roles

You can customize existing or even create completely new roles. This is a powerful feature helping you to fine-tune access to parts of your Moodle. To do that, you should visit the **Administration | Users | Permissions | Define roles** page.

Roles ⑦

Name	Description	Short name	Edit
Administrator	Administrators can usually do anything on the site, in all courses.	admin	✍ ✕ ↓
Course creator	Course creators can create new courses.	coursecreator	✍ ✕ ↑ ↓
Teacher	Teachers can do anything within a course, including changing the activities and grading students.	editingteacher	✍ ✕ ↑ ↓
Non-editing teacher	Non-editing teachers can teach in courses and grade students, but may not alter activities.	teacher	✍ ✕ ↑ ↓
Student	Students generally have fewer privileges within a course.	student	✍ ↑ ↓
Guest	Guests have minimal privileges and usually can not enter text anywhere.	guest	✍ ↑ ↓
Authenticated user	All logged in users.	user	✍ ↑

We have already explained that permissions are calculated based on all roles that a user has within a particular context. Therefore, the most appropriate approach for defining new roles should be based on all roles that a user will have in the higher context and override just a minimal subset of the capabilities.

This is best demonstrated in an example. Let us assume we manage Moodle in a school and apart from students, teachers and other faculty, staff also has course supervisors. We would like to have a set of permissions that permits these supervisors to view all of the courses without actually having to enroll into them while still be unable to modify anything.

We can accomplish this by creating a new role called supervisor. On the **Define roles** page click on the **Add a new role** button.

Fill in the basic data as shown in the following screenshot:

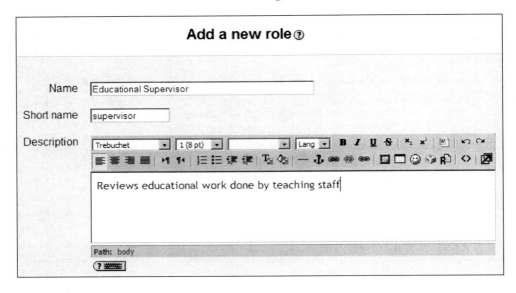

You can see that all capabilities have permission configured to not set. This means that it will not affect the permissions of any existing role. The permission that handles whether a user can see a course or not is called **view course**. Find it in the list of capabilities and click on **Allow**. Finish the process by clicking on the **Add a new role** button.

In order to use this role we should assign it on the system level (visit the **Administration | Users | Permissions | Assign system roles** page) or in case we group courses in several categories, then assign the role in category context. If we want the students to not see the people with this role listed in their course, we should do hidden role assignment. These assignments are only visible to administrators and teachers. On the role assignment page in a course and click on the hidden checkbox (highlighted in the following screenshot).

If we now try to access any course with this user account, the role table would look like this:

User	Context	Role	Capability	Permission
Stan Lee	System	Authenticated user	course_view	not set
		Educational supervisor	course_view	allow
	User			
	Course category			
	Course 1			

The sum of non-set and allow permission is equal to 1 and it implies that user with role supervisor can enter the course.

Overriding roles

The process of overriding existing roles is added to Moodle for cases where we need to slightly modify the existing role only in one context and leave it unchanged in all of the rest. Have in mind that by default only Administrators can modify and create roles. To demonstrate this we will modify the student role within forum context of a course. Go to the course where the forum resides. Click on the **Turn editing on** button and then on the update icon.

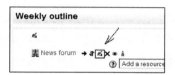

Now on the forum page, click on the **Override permissions** tab:

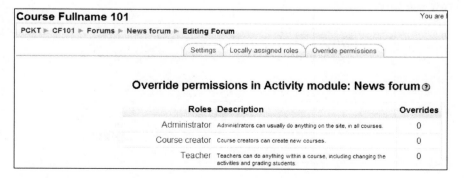

We click on the role we plan on changing and modify the capabilities we want to disable or enable. In this case it would be the student role.

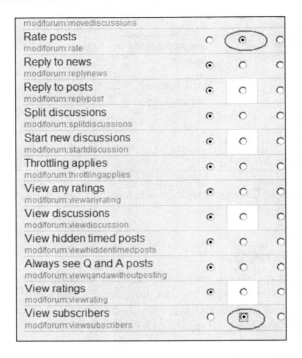

As you can see in the previous screenshot we have highlighted two capabilities:

- **Rate posts**: If enabled it permits a user to rate any message in forum (provided that forum itself is configured with enabled ratings)
- **View subscribers**: If enabled user will be able to see other forum subscribers

We mark the two capabilities enabled by clicking on the second column checkbox and et voila! Our change is done. So when a user logs in next time he would be able to rate the forum posts.

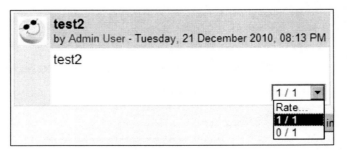

The number of capabilities displayed in the override screen depends on the context in which we perform the change. The system only displays capabilities that can be applied to that context.

 Note that whatever change is made to the existing role will not apply to the users that were logged in at the same time. Change will not be applied until they log out and log in again. This is because Moodle caches all role information upon user log on to reduce performance hit on the database.

Best practices

We will present here a list of recommendations and suggestions to help you improve your security.

Avoid assigning the roles on the system level unless really necessary. Any permission change on the system level affects the entire system and therefore can increase security and maintenance risk. Try to apply roles to the specific part of Moodle where you would like to operate. This is especially important for students and teachers.

Avoid giving more than one role to a user in the same context. A minimalistic approach is the best whenever possible. You should try to fit all your user needs into one role. If you detect a type of user that does not fit completely in any of the existing roles it is most likely time to start creating a new role.

It is better not to change standard roles. In case you wish to introduce a change make a new role based on the standard role and apply your changes to it.

Risky capabilities

All capabilities are marked by risk level value. Moodle defines four risk types—Configuration, XSS, Privacy, and Spam.

- **XSS**: It is a short name for cross-site scripting vulnerability. This vulnerability (when present) may permit a malicious attacker to "inject" client-side script into a web page viewed by other users. This technique is used to obtain data from a user or to circumvent authentication (stealing session ID).

- **Privacy**: This risk denotes a possibility of exposing more information about other users than desired, if an unprotected site can be scraped for user information by Internet bots.

- **Spam**: This level of risk may permit somebody to post unsolicited content either directly within a platform or by sending personal messages to other users.

Here is the list of the several capabilities with highest risk danger. Remember that you can access these (and other) capabilities within a specific role by visiting the **Administration | Users | Permissions | Define roles** page.

- **Create new blog entries**: With this capability, users are permitted to create new blog entries. It is marked with spam risk since it can be abused by a malicious user to generate and post spam content. Authenticated user role has this setting enabled; hence all users by default can create blog posts.

  To increase the security we recommend disabling blog feature completely unless it is necessary for your educational process. To disable blog visit **Administration | Security | Site policies**, locate **Blog visibility** and set it to **Disable blog system completely**.

  An alternative to this would be disabling this capability in Authenticated user role and modifying one of the other existing roles to include it in case we just want to limit which users can blog.

- **Create users on restore**: This capability allows a user to create new users while importing a course/platform backup. By default, it is permitted only for Administrator role. You should not enable this capability within other roles unless you are creating separate administration roles. This capability has been introduced in Moodle 1.9.8 in order to prevent security issues with user data. All users are advised to upgrade as soon as possible.

- **Change site configuration and Allowed to do anything**: These two are obviously for administrators only. It is extremely risky to give these capabilities to too many users as it gives full access to everything. Keep it within Administrator role.

- **Change own password**: This is a potentially dangerous capability. If any user account is breached by a malicious user he can modify the password and effectively prevent the real user from using the platform. We recommend disabling this capability at least for the student roles. However, this would put additional burden on the support staff in case any student forgets his credentials.

- **View participants (system level)**: With this capability enabled a user can see all user accounts (**Administration | Users | Accounts | Browse list of users**). It is not set by default in any role outside the Administrator role. We recommend leaving it as such.

- **View participants (course level)**: With this capability enabled a user can see all participants of a course (**<course> | Participants**). By default student role has this setting enabled. If you want to isolate users from peeking into profiles of each other you should modify student role and change permission to **not set**. This would also remove participants block from course view.

- **Backup user data**: By default this capability is enabled only for Administrator role. We recommend to leave it like that and to protect all such accounts with strong passwords. The reason why this is dangerous is that through course backup a malicious user could easily obtain all user data together with passwords.

Summary

In this chapter we learned about the Moodle permission system and the explained concepts on which it is built. We gave a detailed example of permission calculation and influence of context precedence on the final outcome. In the last part we described best practices for using and applying roles within Moodle. We also presented the capabilities that may expose the system to a security risk and recommended ways of using them.

In the next chapter we will focus on protection against robots and spam-bots.

6
Protection Against Bots

Search engines are one of the great inventions that helped the Internet grow and become what it is today. Any powerful tool can be (and usually is) a double-edged sword. With search engines we the common users, can find almost anything that is of our personal interest, but as a website owner and/or administrator we must know what amount of information is available to the general public. If that amount surpasses our intentional or allowed boundaries, then we must know how to detect such instances and remedy the situation. In this chapter we will focus on the following topics:

- Internet bots — types and dangers
- Protecting Moodle from undesired search bots
- Protection against spam bots
- Protection against brute force dictionary attacks

Internet bots

Internet bots are software applications that run automated tasks applied to any content publicly available on the Internet. Usually they perform tasks that are repetitive and trivial at a much higher speed than any human being can do. We will outline the most common uses here.

Search engine content indexing

This is a task performed by all major search engines. Their bots scan the web all the time reading publicly available content and indexing it for searching purposes. This basically applies to any textual content although multimedia files can also be indexed by their name and description.

Harvesting email addresses

These bots analyze public content of web sites and extract any email addresses, thus generating a mailing list of potential recipients. To understand why somebody would need a list of email addresses we need to understand the concept of spam. Any form of unsolicited message received through some electronic service is considered spam. These messages usually contain advertisements for various products or services. The most widely known variant of spam is email spam. In order to distribute these messages spammers need mail addresses. One way of obtaining them is by running email harvester bots.

Website scraping

Web scraping is a computer software technique of extracting information from the websites. That generally means copying and potential transformation of unstructured web content into a more manageable form for some kind of automated analysis. Common uses of web scraping are making a complete offline copy of the site content (stealing course information), obtaining personal user information (name, address, email, etc.) that can later be used for sending spam or for selling it to other mail advertising companies.

Spam generators

Electronic spam has many forms and spammers use any kind of messaging/ publishing system to promote their agenda. Internet bots that automatically create spam content are called spam generators. Any blog, CMS, forum, and internal messaging system are a potential target for this kind of attack. For example, if you open your Moodle for self-registration and do not apply all of the protection measures you leave a door open for a spam attack. Specially crafted bot can create several fake accounts and start posting unsolicited messages in all available forums or by using personal messaging system.

Protecting Moodle from unwanted search bots

Every access to our Moodle website generates traffic, from requesting computer to the server and the other way around. Web server consumes CPU, memory, and other machine resources to generate and deliver desired content to the user. As with anything else in our physical world, all resources are finite and usage of those resources generates cost. We want to employ our platform's resources only to the desirable, legal requests. Since there is no functional difference between page requests made by some automated software and live users, we need to know that giving free access to anybody will implicate higher maintenance costs, open a potential security hole, and most likely incur a performance hit and reduce the availability of the website. This means that we must be aware of the kind of requests that can be made by legal or illegal bots on our Moodle platform.

Search engines

Publicly available websites used for searching of the World Wide Web are generally referred to as search engines. The most common and most widely known example of such a website is Google (of course there are others like Bing, Yahoo, Baidu, Yandex, AltaVista, etc.). Most of the search engines employ Internet bots that scrape keywords from raw HTML content and generate data cache storage which is later used to generate a response list to a user search request. To determine whether our site is indexed by some search engine we can use **site** keyword. For example, typing **site: www.packtpub.com** in Google will produce a list of all indexed pages for that site.

That is the easiest way to determine the level of exposure of your website on Google, and the process is similar with the other search engines.

Moodle and search engines

Moodle has basic support for handling several public search engines. Supported engines are Google, Yahoo, AltaVista, and Bing. For the Intranet purposes Moodle also supports Zoom search engine from WrenSoft.

This means that if we configure Moodle to permit external indexing by search engines they will be permitted to scan the entire site without the need to log in.

In order to enable your Moodle to permit indexing of the front page and any other publicly available resource, you need to go to the **Administration | Security | Site policies** and check the option **Open to Google**.

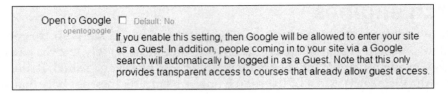

Even though the option refers to Google only, it actually applies to all supported search engines.

Moodle access check

Moodle has a well defined process of granting or denying access to a user. This is not so well documented and since it is important to understand how access check actually works we will explain it in depth here. As a result you will know how to properly configure your system and open just the parts you want to have opened to the general public.

By default a Moodle instance permits anybody to enter on a front page and into any activity, resource, or course that permits free entrance to guest users.

To configure a specific course open for guests, visit the course settings page **<course short name> | Edit course settings** and in the **Availability** section mark **Guest access** with option **Allow guests without key**. This means that anybody will be able to enter into such a course and browse its content as a guest user.

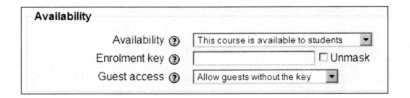

Guest access in Moodle is permitted by default. You can configure that feature if you visit **Administration | Users | Authentication | Manage authentication** and set the **Guest login button** to show or hide.

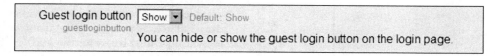

One final option completes the set that controls the level of openness you want to give to your Moodle. That is **Force users to login**. With that option configured nobody can access anything within the platform unless he logs in.

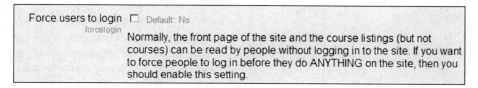

And here is the decision process that Moodle makes when a user wants to access the platform:

Force users to log in	Guest login button	Open to Google	Security level
Yes	Hide	No	This is the highest security level. Nobody can enter the site without valid credentials. No bot will be able to enter the site. This is a recommended setting for any Moodle instance hosted on the Internet.
Yes	Hide	Yes	With this configuration set, only users with valid credentials and allowed search engines can enter the website. Search engine bot will be able to see anything on the front page and any course marked for guest access. This is a recommended way of configuring platform in a case where we want the search engine to index publicly available content. (There are some additional security concerns that should be considered—more on that a bit later.)

Force users to log in	Guest login button	Open to Google	Security level
Yes	Show	No	This is misleading configuration because we have guest access enabled but disabled search engines. This however does not actually stop any bot from activating **Guest login** button and entering the site as guest user. This is therefore not a recommended setting.
Yes	Show	Yes	This configuration set still asks for users to be logged in but enables both guest access and permitted search engines. Not recommended if you do not want to expose your site to the public eye.
No	Show	Yes	These configurations leave open the front page of the site for anybody to see together with any content open for guest access. These are generally not recommended settings for public websites. They are more appropriate for internal Intranet use.
No	Show	No	
No	Hide	Yes	
No	Hide	No	This is the most appropriate configuration for opening front page to search engines without forcing users to log in and giving any additional access within the site.

There are serious security concerns related to the **Open to Google** setting. The reason for this is the way Moodle checks whether a permitted search engine bot is trying to access the site. Every HTTP request contains some information about the client. This information is formed through so-called HTTP headers.

 In HTTP protocol requests, header fields contain operating parameters of the request or response. Through headers we inform the web server what resource (page) we want, what is our identifier, and so on.

The HTTP header used for identifying the source of the request is called **User-Agent**. User-Agent is a header destined to identify the client software that is making request. All web browsers and well behaving bots have standardized User-Agent values.

The problem, of course, is that it is extremely easy to modify this value within your browser or within your web bot and thus impersonate another browser or bot. For example, in order to permit Google bot to enter inside the site, Moodle checks whether a value of User-Agent header contains the value Google bot. In case that is true, then this request is allowed and the bot is automatically logged into platform as a guest user.

To demonstrate how easy it is to pass this protection I will use Mozilla Firefox 3.6. You can customize the User-Agent value for that browser. To do that in the location bar, type **about:config** and inside the filter field enter **agent**.

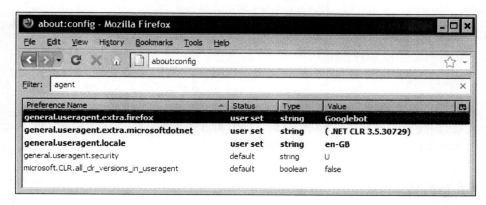

Locate the key **general.useragent.extra.firefox** and double-click on it to set value **Googlebot** (it is case-sensitive). Restart the browser and open your Moodle which is configured to allow search engine bots. You will notice that you are logged in as a guest user just by opening the front page.

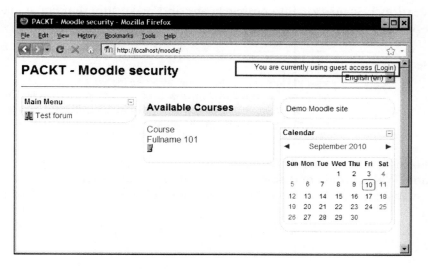

This clearly demonstrates how easy it is to bypass this protection. Therefore whenever possible, configure your Moodle with the recommended highest security settings (see table).

Protection against spam bots

In the previous section we covered bots that analyze raw content of the website but additional steps are needed to prevent malicious scripts from automatically creating spam content within Moodle itself. Moodle has four elements that are targeted by spam bots:

- User profiles
- E-mail self-registration
- User blogs
- Internal messaging system

Let us explain each targeted segment in depth and propose the most adequate security measures you as an administrator can apply.

User profiles

Every user account within Moodle has profile. A profile must contain username, password, name, surname, e-mail address, city, and country, while all the other fields are considered optional. The presence of an e-mail address presents a goldmine for any spam bot. Therefore it is essential to protect access to this information only to the logged-in users. Luckily, Moodle offers this as a configuration option. Visit the **Administration | Security | Site policies** page and make sure that **Force users to login for profiles** is checked, which by default is.

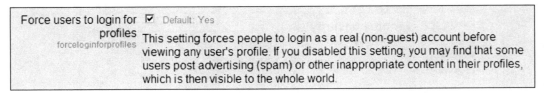

Force users to login for profiles
forceloginforprofiles

☑ Default: Yes

This setting forces people to login as a real (non-guest) account before viewing any user's profile. If you disabled this setting, you may find that some users post advertising (spam) or other inappropriate content in their profiles, which is then visible to the whole world.

Some spammers also use the description field for propagating unwanted information. We can prevent displaying descriptions of users who are not yet enrolled in any course. Visit the Site policies page and check **Profile for enrolled users only**.

As an ultimate measure you can completely disable profile editing by all users except administrators. That is done in authentication module configuration (see Chapter 4 for more details).

E-mail-based self-registration

We already explained the proper configuration for e-mail-based self-registration in case you need it on your website (see Chapter 4 for more details). That authentication method is a potential door to malicious users and bots to start producing spam within the Moodle. It is always safer to completely disable it. You can do that by visiting **Administration | Users | Authentication | Manage authentication** and setting **Self registration** to **Disable**.

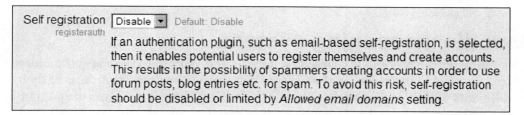

User blogs

Blog is a shortened name for web log and represents sort of an electronic online diary that can be a complete website or part of a more complex website. Blogs consist of entries that are chronologically ordered and can contain text and other multimedia content. Because of that they are ideal for generating a wide variety of spam content. In Moodle blogs are enabled by default site-wide and are mutually visible to all users within the platform. Blogs can have five levels of visibility:

1. **The world can read entries set to be world-accessible**: This opens all blog entries on the site for anybody to see (unless you have the **Force to login** option set to **yes**).

2. **All site users can see all blog entries**: This is the default setting and is usually a good enough setting for general purpose uses, provided that you want to have blogs enabled for your users.

3. **Users can see blog for people who share course**: This setting is good for cases where you want to isolate groups of users on the course level.

4. **Users can see blog for people who share a group**: This setting is good for cases where you want to isolate blog visibility for users within the same group.

5. **Users can see their own blog**: Not very useful option.

In case you need blogs for your users we recommend limiting internal visibility to either course or group. That way you minimize potential exposure to spam and at the same time have working blog system. If you do not plan on having blog — disable it! That can be done on Site policies page.

Moodle messaging system

Messaging within Moodle is enabled by default. It is not limited to a specific course or role. Logged in users can send messages between each others regardless of their enrollments within particular course(s) or their roles. There is a danger of spam in case a real account is hacked (somebody discovered or guessed the password) and then using that, account spammer can send mails to all users within the platform. In such cases administrator will have to react and disable or delete such an account. It is possible to completely disable the messaging system by going to site policies page and unchecking **Enable messaging system**. Another option is to limit messaging by making it read-only for all users except for some particular role. This can be done by modifying **Authenticated user** role on the system level.

Go to **Administration | Users | Permissions | Define roles** page and click on edit for **Authenticated user** role.

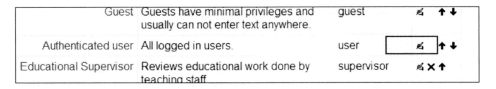

Locate the permission **Send messages to any user** and set it to **Not set**.

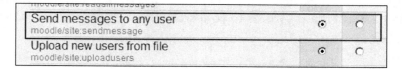

As a result of this change all users, except those who have Administrator role on the system level, will be unable to send messages. You can further extend changes and mark this setting for another existing role or create a new one and that way have other group of users without administrative privileges and capability to send messages.

Cleaning up spam

As of Moodle 1.9.4, there is a Spam Cleaner report. To use it, visit the **Administration | Reports | Spam cleaner** page:

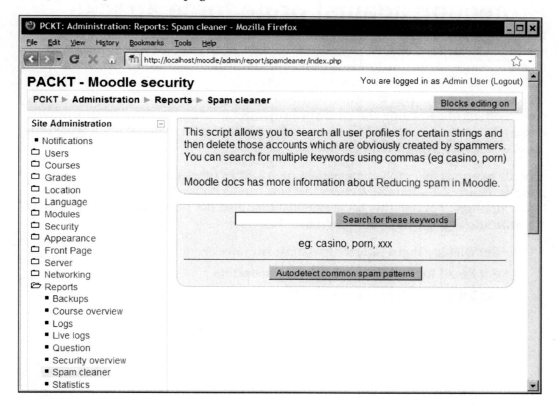

This report searches for the most common spam keywords within user profiles. The elements that are subjected to test are profile description and blog posts. You can enter a list of the keywords to be searched for or use predefined list.

Results of searching user profiles containing: bad		
User	**Description**	**Operation**
1 studen stud • Lumberton • US • sta@acme.com	bad	Delete user Ignore
	Delete all these user accounts	

Protection against brute force attacks

In cryptography, a brute force attack or exhaustive key search is a strategy that can in theory be used against any encrypted data by an attacker who is unable to take advantage of any weakness in an encryption system that would otherwise make his task easier. It involves systematically checking all possible keys until the correct key is found. This is a quite common technique that basically probes various combinations of username and passwords in order to enter the site. The general reason for doing this is to obtain access to the platform and then use it for generating spam or for harvesting user information.

Moodle has no active protection against such attacks other than strong password policies. However, administrators or teachers can be notified for all cases of failed logon attempts. To configure these notifications, visit the **Administration | Security | Notifications page** and configure it like this:

- Set **Display login failures** to **Administrators**
- Set **Email login failures** to **All administrators**
- Set **Threshold for email notifications** to **10**

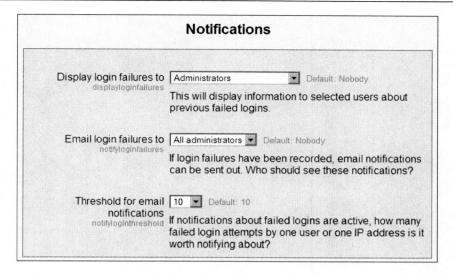

For this to work you must have properly configured mail support within Moodle and have cron job up and running. As a result, every time somebody tries to log in using the same username more than 10 times or tries to log in from same IP, an administrator will receive an e-mail that is generated every time cron is executed. That can be a good source of information and valid hint for any administrator to react by either blocking the specific IP or blocking some user account.

Summary

In this chapter you learned about types of Internet bots: What their purpose is and how to protect your instance of Moodle against them. We outlined search engine support embedded into Moodle and what level of exposure you can enable or disable according to your specific needs. We outlined all weak points within the Moodle that can be used for generating and propagating spam content. We also demonstrated tools and techniques for detecting and cleaning spam generated inside the platform and the notification system designed to inform us if anybody is probing the system for detecting passwords. Our next stop is user files security within Moodle.

7
Securing User Files

In this chapter we will focus on files submitted by any course participant, any kind of security issues involved with that and ways of protecting your system. The material will be covered in the following order:

- Uploading files into Moodle
- Dangers and pitfalls
- Anti-virus and Moodle

Uploading files into Moodle

In an educational process oriented towards digital systems lot of things must be adapted to the new way of interaction between a student and a teacher. One of the most notable changes is the way results of particular assignments are treated. For example, if a teacher wants to assign a task to write a paper about medieval English literature for all participants in a course he would create an "Upload single file" activity.

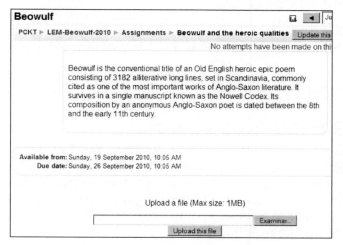

By adding this and other kinds of activities that require the user to submit various types of files, poses potential security problems. Before going into more details let us expose all points of file submitting in Moodle available to the students and teachers.

How Moodle stores files

The files not part of the core platform, files that are dynamic—changeable nature, are stored within `Moodledata` directory. Every course within Moodle has a sub directory within Moodledata. The name of the directory is identical to the value of the course ID within database. For example, if course ID is 4 it will have folder `<path to Moodledata>/Moodledata/4`. You can see the course ID within the URL as a URL parameter.

Every type of content uploaded to the specific course is stored within its Moodledata directory.

Points of submitting user files

Within Moodle course there are five places where user can upload files and they are:

- WYSIWYG HTMLArea editor
- Glossary
- Upload a single file or Advanced uploading of files activity
- Forum
- Database activity module

WYSIWYG HTMLArea editor

WYSIWYG is an acronym for **What You See Is What You Get**. The term is used to describe an editor or other kind of tool in which the content displayed during editing appears very similar if not identical to the final output. Moodle comes with included WYSIWYG editor intended for creating rich content pages (formatted text, embedded images, links to external and/or internal resources, etc.). That editor comes with the facility for inserting images.

This feature permits uploading ANY kind of file as long as it fits within the system limits for maximum file size (upload_max_filesize directive in php.ini). This is the reason this option is so dangerous. A user can easily upload a virus-infected file which can potentially be opened by a teacher or other users. It is worth noting that ONLY teachers and administrators can upload files in this way. Common users can only link to the external files. A Moodle admin can also control the limit for the maximum upload file size setting this limit in the Site Administration block in the section: **Security | Site Policies | Maximum uploaded file size,** choosing the desired limit. Also the teacher can configure this setting in his course using the Maximum upload size configuration located at the course administration block.

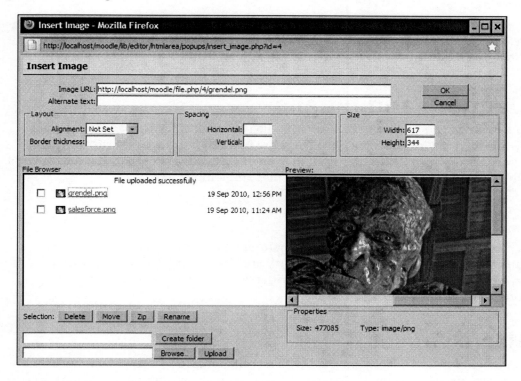

A glossary can be placed within any course by a teacher or administrator and allows all participants to create and maintain a custom list of term definitions. During the process of creation of new term an attachment can be specified by a user. No file type limitations are present other than the size of the file.

Upload single file simple/advanced assignment

This type of assignment is commonly used for treating tasks that require students to present written papers in electronic format. Usually students produce a document in some word processor or PDF format suitable for submitting. However, there are no limitations as to which format can be uploaded.

Forum

Forums are an excellent way of initiating discussion between participants in a course. Everybody within a course with adequate permissions can add a new discussion topic or respond to an existing one. Unless explicitly disabled, all forums by default permit users to attach a file together with their message and also insert an image if WYSIWYG editor is enabled.

Database activity

Database activity module permits a teacher to create a bank of record entries made by students. It can contain anything—files, short or long texts, mixed content, etc. What this module permits is to specify file upload fields.

Dangers and pitfalls

The main danger related to the way Moodle implements file uploads is potential distribution of virus infected files. There are two major groups of viruses—classic binary virus which distributes itself in form of executable program, and macro virus which spreads itself through document files and templates.

Classic viruses

A computer program capable of copying itself by infecting other executables during its execution is called a **virus**. They are always targeted to a particular type of Operating System, so viruses written for Microsoft Windows will not run on Apple OS X and vice versa.

Macro viruses

Document files are usually infected with so-called macro viruses. **Macro viruses** are computer viruses written in document application programming macro language. Unlike standard viruses which infect executable files (other programs), these ones infect documents and document templates. Document types that are most affected are those produced by Microsoft Office suite. The most affected apps are Word, Excel, and PowerPoint.

Applying protection measures

The main question here is what we as an administrator can do in terms of platform configuration to prevent the spreading of these kinds of files. Here is some advice that can help you in making your website more secure.

Disable WYSIWIG editor if you do not need it

If your users do not need the advanced editing features of WYSIWIG editor in general, then you can disable it globally. That way you are essentially blocking the file upload through the insert image feature for the teachers and administrators and external file linking for common users. To do that visit **Administration | Appearance | HTML editor** and uncheck the **Use HTML editor** option.

Enable file upload in forums only when you really need it

As we have previously mentioned, by default in any forum users can attach files to their posts. We recommend disabling attachments on the platform level and enabling them only in the specific forums where you might need that feature. To disable forum attachments globally, visit the **Administration | Modules | Activities | Forum** page and change the option **Maximum attachment size** to **0 bytes**.

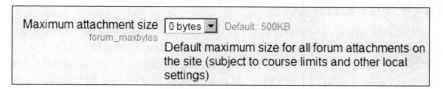

Setting it like this means that any new forum created in any course will have attachments disabled by default.

Anti-virus and Moodle

Aware of the dangers present in permitting users to upload files, developers of Moodle decided to integrate anti-virus support into their platform. Being an Open Source platform they opted for open source solution, In this case it is ClamAV. **ClamAV** is released under GPL license (like Moodle) and is specifically designed for e-mail scanning on mail gateways/servers. Integration in Moodle with ClamAV is done in such way that every time a virus is detected administrator receives the notification through e-mail. Virus detection is integrated with file upload. Any part of Moodle that permits file upload will perform virus check if it is enabled and configured properly.

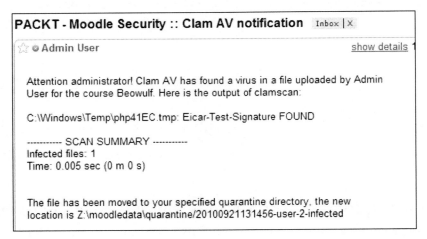

Next, we will show step by step instructions for setting up ClamAV on both Linux and Windows.

ClamAV on Linux

ClamAV was developed originally for UNIX and derivatives (like Linux), so Linux can be considered like native platform for this software. Unfortunately, CentOS 5 does not include packages for ClamAV. Fortunately, there is an external package repository that hosts CentOS packages. It is a repository called RPMforge maintained by Dag Wieers.

To set up new repository execute this from the command line for 32-bit:

```
rpm -Uhv http://apt.sw.be/redhat/el5/en/i386/rpmforge/RPMS/rpmforge-
release-0.3.6-1.el5.rf.i386.rpm
```

Or the following one for a 64-bit version of OS:

```
rpm -Uhv http://apt.sw.be/redhat/el5/en/x86_64/rpmforge/RPMS//rpmforge-
release-0.3.6-1.el5.rf.x86_64.rpm
```

 Package names can change in time. In order to install the latest version of the repository correctly, visit the Dag Wieers home page at http://dag.wieers.com/rpm/FAQ.php#B.

After executing this command, open the file located at /etc/yum.repos.d/ rpmforge.repo and change the following line:

```
enabled = 1
```

to:

```
enabled = 0
```

By doing this change we are explicitly disabling this repository, thus preventing anybody from accidentally installing anything that might overwrite default packages and/or libraries from standard CentOS repositories.

Now we are ready to install ClamAV with this command:

```
yum -y --enablerepo=rpmforge install clamav clamav-db clamd
```

Update virus signature database by executing this from the command line:

```
/usr/bin/freshclam
```

Apart from basic scanning tools we also installed clamd. It is anti-virus service (daemon) that speeds up scanning of the files substantially when used and reduces CPU utilization which is very important on the web server. To start it, execute this:

```
/sbin/service start clamd
```

Everything else is already configured. Every day the scheduled task will be executed that updates virus signature database (cron job) and clamd service will start automatically during system boot process.

Configuring Moodle

We are ready to configure Moodle to use ClamAV. To do that visit the **Administration | Security | Anti-Virus** page and do the following:

1. Check option **Use clam AV on uploaded files**.
2. Set **clam AV path** to /usr/bin/clamdscan.
3. Set **On clam AV failure option** to **Treat files as OK**.

ClamAV on Windows

ClamAV has several builds for Windows, some free and other commercial. We will use the build provided directly from the official page. Unfortunately, there is neither support nor any help available that comes with this distribution whatsoever. So we must do much more in order to make it work properly.

Downloading

Visit the download page for Windows binary package on ClamAV website `http://www.clamav.net/lang/en/download/packages/packages-win32/`. On that page you can find out where the latest version for Windows is located. At the time of writing this book, latest version was 0.96.2 available here at `http://downloads.sourceforge.net/project/clamav/clamav/win32/ClamAV-0.96.2-win32.zip`.

Open the elevated command prompt and execute this:

```
bitsadmin /transfer getclamav /priority HIGH http://downloads.
sourceforge.net/project/clamav/clamav/win32/ClamAV-0.96.2-win32.zip Z:\
temp\ClamAV-0.96.2-win32.zip
```

Now create a directory structure where you plan on storing Clam AV and apply appropriate permissions:

```
mkdir Z:\clamav
icacls Z:\clamav /Q /T /grant moodle:(OI)(CI)(RX)
mkdir Z:\clamav\db
mkdir Z:\clamav\tmp
mkdir Z:\moodledata\quarantine
```

With the above commands we created a `clamav` directory and assigned read/execute permissions to Moodle user, which we specially created for running Moodle website. This is important as PHP is being executed using user Moodle and therefore that user must have sufficient permissions to execute ClamAV. Sub directory `db` will be used to store virus definition database and `tmp` for antivirus service processing.

Extract downloaded file using Compression support in Windows Explorer to `Z:\clamav`. To do this, open Windows Explorer and navigate to `Z:\temp`. Right-click on the file you just downloaded and choose **Extract All** option.

Configuring clamd service

It is essential to use clamd service for scanning as it is much faster than using plain command line scanner. The reason for this is the way these two are implemented. Command line virus scanner clamscan loads virus signature database every time before performing scan, and just by doing that it uses several seconds and clamd is permanently resident. Therefore, it loads virus signature database once during startup or when it detects that update was applied which usually happens once per day. Service configuration is performed with clamd.conf file. This file must be located in the same folder where ClamAV engine (libclamav.dll) is stored. In our case it is the same folder where we installed ClamAV — z:\clamav.

The content of our configuration clamd.conf file is as follows:

```
LogFile Z:\clamav\clamd.log
DatabaseDirectory Z:\clamav\db
LogFileMaxSize 0
LogTime yes
TemporaryDirectory Z:\clamav\tmp
TCPSocket 3310
TCPAddr 127.0.0.1
MaxConnectionQueueLength 30
ReadTimeout 300
SelfCheck 0
```

We define where the log file of the service will be stored, where is the virus signature database, what is the temporary folder for scanning and the port and IP address through which service can be contacted by it's client (clamdscan).

Next step in this process is setting up clamd as Windows service. Unfortunately, clamd.exe itself is not prepared to be executed as Windows service, but we have alternatives. Microsoft offers custom resource kit tool for transforming common executable into full fledged service. It is called SrvAny.

SrvAny is a part of Windows Server 2003 Resource Kit. You can download it free of charge from the Microsoft website using this URL http://www.microsoft.com/downloads/en/details.aspx?FamilyID=9D467A69-57FF-4AE7-96EE-B18C4790CFFD.

When installing this package on Windows 2008 you will be notified by OS that this software was not designed to work reliably. Acknowledge that fact but continue installing the product. Choose custom folder as a destination. We recommend `C:\rkit`.

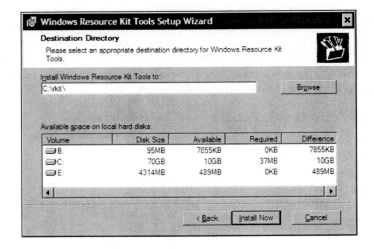

After finishing the installation, open elevated command prompt and execute:

```
sc create clamd type= own start= auto binpath= C:\rkit\srvany.exe
```

This creates a new windows service entry pointing to SrvAny executable. Now we need to configure this service. Initiate the Run option from the Start menu:

And in the dialog type **regedit**:

Locate the key `HKEY_LOCAL_MACHINE\SYSTEM\CurrentControlSet\Services\`
`clamd`.

In there add new key called **Parameters**. Inside that key add new string value called
Application and as a value set location to `clamd.exe - Z:\clamav\clamd.exe.`

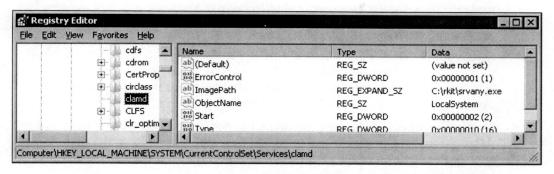

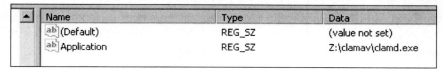

With this ends the configuration of anti-virus service.

Setting up virus signature database update

Every day a handful of new viruses appear worldwide. All updates are eventually
added to the ClamAV central database. It is important to have the updated
version because it helps us detect all the latest threats. Updates are performed by
freshclam. This program connects to the location where updated files are located
and downloads them to a local hard drive. Freshclam configuration is located in
`freshclam.conf`. It is to be placed in the same location with `clamd.conf` — `Z:\`
`clamav`. The content of our `freshclam.conf` is as follows:

```
DatabaseDirectory Z:\clamav\db
DatabaseMirror clamav.edebris.com
DatabaseMirror database.clamav.net
NotifyClamd Z:\clamav\clamd.conf
UpdateLogFile Z:\clamav\update.log
```

In order to understand the configuration file better, we offer some quick pointers:

- **Databasedirectory** defines the location to which freshclam should download the updated files.

- **DatabaseMirror** defines the location where freshclam should look for updated files. Configuration file should have at least one location defined but it is preferred to have two or more to ensure successful download. To obtain the list of available mirrors visit the `http://www.clamav.net/mirrors.html` page. On that page you will find up-to date list of active virus database mirrors. We recommend that you choose servers that are geographically closer to your server location. You should always put the central server (`database.clamav.net`) at the end of the list.

- **NotifyClamd** is used to ensure that clamd service is notified that there is a database update available and to reload new definitions from the disk. We specify the location of the clamd configuration file so that freshclam knows how to communicate with the service.

- **UpdateLogFile** defines a file where freshclam stores outcome of his actions. It is considered a good practice to have this file since it can help determine source of any potential problem with updates.

To verify whether this configuration works, open command prompt, go into ClamAV directory, and execute freshclam. If everything works OK you will have a latest virus signature database ready for the use.

Scheduling updates

We are not finished yet with freshclam. Remember that we need to update virus signatures every day in order to have highest level of protection. In Linux one uses cron for such purposes but in Windows we can use Task Scheduler.

Start the Task Scheduler by choosing option **Start menu | Administrative Tools | Task Scheduler**.

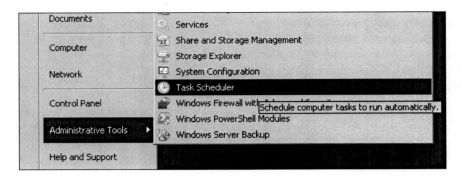

Choose **Create task** option from the left command pane.

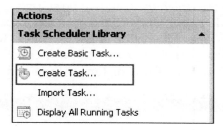

In the initial screen we need to set the task name and the way it is executed. In the **Name** field enter **ClamAV update**. Make sure to check **Run whether user is logged or not** and **Do not store password...** option.

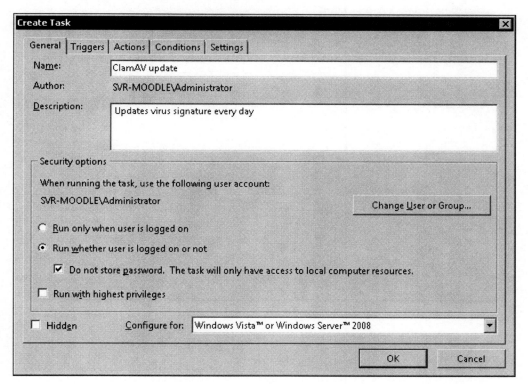

Switch to the **Triggers** tab in the same dialog and click on **New...** button. We are defining the condition under which the task will be started. In the **Begin the task** field, choose **On a schedule** value. Under **Settings** check repetition period to **Daily** and set period to one day. I leave the value of the **Start** field to your personal choice. General practice is to choose period of day with low user activity — usually around midnight. Check option **Stop task if it runs longer than** and set it to **4 hours**.

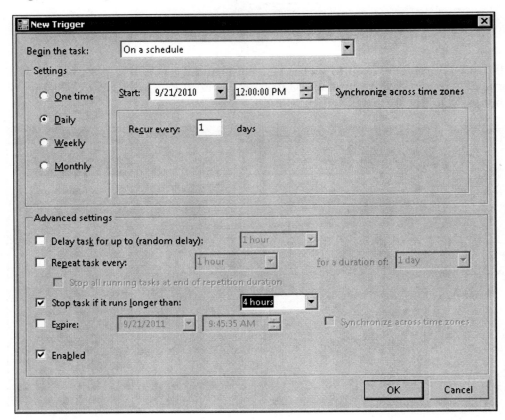

Confirm the setting by clicking the **OK** button and switch to the **Actions** tab. An action in this case would be execution of freshclam. Click on the **New...** button. In the **New Action** dialog set **Action** field to **Start a program**. In **Program/script** put the location to your `freshclam.exe`—`Z:\clamav\freshclam.exe`, and in the **Add arguments** fields place following text—`config-file=<path to freshclam.conf>`, which would be in our case—`config-file=Z:\clamav\freshclam.conf`. This is just a safety guard to ensure that proper configuration is used by freshclam.

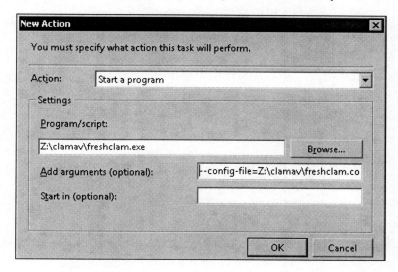

Switch to the **Conditions** tab and check **Start only if the following network connection is available** and choose **Any connection**. With this setting we are making sure to execute the task only when the server is actually connected to the network.

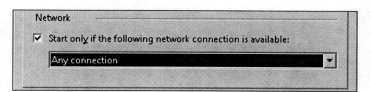

Finally, switch to the **Settings** tab and check **Allow task to be run on demand**. Also activate **If the task fails, restart every:** and set it to **1 minute**, and set number of retries to 3. Check **Stop the task if it runs longer than** and set it to **4 hours**. **If the running task does not end when requested force it to stop** is something you should activate too. With all that configured click on **OK**.

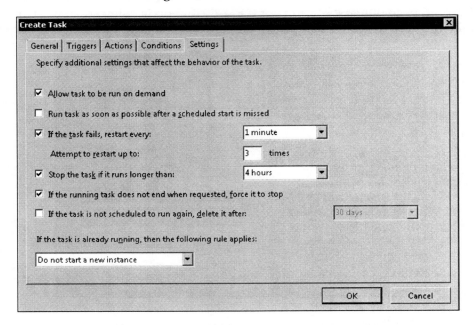

Good work! You just configured your automatic updates for ClamAV.

Final steps

We are almost at the end of anti-virus configuration in Windows. To activate checking, start the clamd service. Open the elevated command prompt and execute:

```
net start clamd
```

Open the **Administration | Security | Anti-Virus** page within Moodle and configure it as shown in the following screenshot:

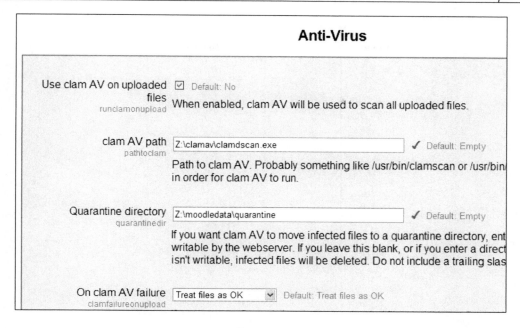

To test ClamAV functioning within the Moodle download `eicar.txt`, which is a standard anti-virus test file from `http://www.eicar.org/download/eicar.com.txt`, try to upload it in some course. You should see something like this:

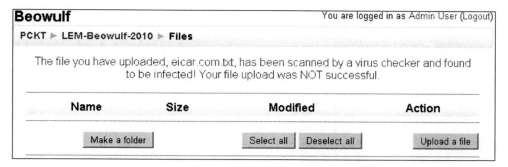

Summary

In this chapter we exposed potential vulnerabilities related to uploaded files by users and some advice on how to remedy the situation. We also explained how to install and configure ClamAV on both Linux and Windows. You will have a much safer working environment after applying everything from this chapter to your instance in Moodle.

8

Securing Moodle Data

When we talk about Moodle data we are referring to both the user and the course information and binary files that are within the platform. In the previous chapter we were talking about user files only. Now we will focus our attention to the protection and separation of internal Moodle data between valid platform users. The topics we will cover include:

- User information protection
- Course information protection

User information protection

Every user within Moodle has a profile which can contain information we may or may not want to show to other users, or at least not to all of them. The level of exposure will depend on the privacy policy we want to adopt. For example, we may want to completely isolate users within a course so that nobody knows who else is participating, or we may want to expose just the user names and nothing else, and so on. Let us first describe how Moodle handles presentation of user profiles. This is important as it will expose internal workings of that subsystem and identify all access points and ways of disabling them if that is what we want to do.

User profile page

User profile page is used to define personal information about a user within a Moodle. It can contain name, surname, address, telephone, etc. The user profile page is reached by `<Moodle URL>/user/view.php?id=<userid>&course=<courseid>` where `userid` and `courseid` are identifiers of user and course as they are stored in database. This is how Moodle determines whether to show or not the profile page for a particular user:

Logged-on user	User to see	Condition	Show profile
User	Other user	Other user is teacher in at least one course	yes
		User is teacher in at least one course	yes
		User has View user profiles capability enabled in current context	yes
		None of the above	no
User	User	None	yes

 When we say teacher we refer to the Moodle roles Teacher and Non-editing teacher.

Reaching profile page

There are several ways a user can reach the profile page for a particular user. We are presenting them here in order to help the administrator to block potentially unwanted access points to user information.

People block

Every course upon creation gets a set of predefined blocks. One of these blocks is the people block. When present and visible it gives every user an opportunity to browse all users participating in the current course.

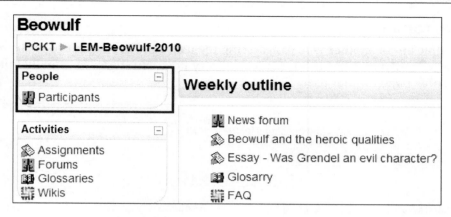

This block is visible to any user that has the View participants capability enabled. This capability exists for system and course level. In Moodle 1.9.8 and later, by default this capability is enabled only for the Administrator role on both levels. That way no user other than Administrator will be able to see participants on the system level or in specific course.

If by any chance you use an older version of Moodle, then most likely you have this capability enabled on the course level for all standard roles except for guest and authenticated user. Unless you want to open privacy policy on your site we recommend you to disable this capability.

Visit the **Administration | Users | Permissions | Define roles** page, then locate and modify that capability by setting it to "Not set". Apply this at least on the Student role.

Forum topics

Forum topic offers another way of accessing the user profile. Regardless of the forum type, Moodle displays the author name for every post. This name is actually linked to the profile page for that user.

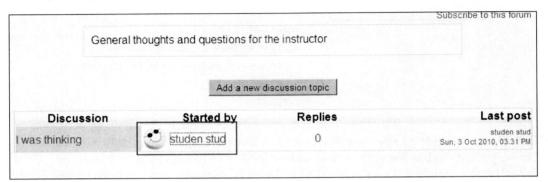

Messaging system

Moodle offers a messaging system for internal communications between users. The Messaging system can be accessed from three locations—personal profile page, platform front page, and course content page.

Moodle page	Conditions	Displayed
Profile page	Send message to any user capability is enabled	Yes
Front page	Message block is added by Administrator	Yes
Course content page	Message block is added to the course by Administrator or teacher	Yes

If any of these conditions are fulfilled users will be able to access the messaging system. By default none of these conditions are present for Students and therefore there is no danger of any privacy intrusion. However, it is a common practice in various installations of Moodle to add a messaging block to one or more courses. Any user will be able to communicate with other users within same context (course). The problem with messaging is that it enables any user to locate any other user registered in the platform. We can demonstrate this easily. Open the messaging dialog and switch to the **Search** tab. In the **Name** field enter one letter and press the **Search** button. You will get ALL user accounts that have the specified letter either in name or surname as a result.

The search result apart from the actual names of the users also offers a direct link to their personal profile.

This is a potentially dangerous feature that can expose more information than we are willing to permit. If messaging is called from a context in which the users have permission to view user profiles he will be able to see any profile in the system. This way user names and profiles are completely open. There is no way to modify this behavior (listing all users) other than disabling the messaging system. Having a messaging system enabled can be a problem if you have a malicious user within your system that wants to get names of all users or a spam-bot that wishes to harvest e-mail addresses (see Chapter 6). That is the reason we should do something about that.

Protecting user profile information

We have several options available for protecting access to private information located in personal user profile. You can choose one that is most appropriate for your particular use case.

Limit information exposed to all users

If we do not have a problem exposing some information of the user in their profile then we can then just hide some fields. To do that visit the **Administration | Users | Permissions | User policies** page and locate the **Hide user fields** section.

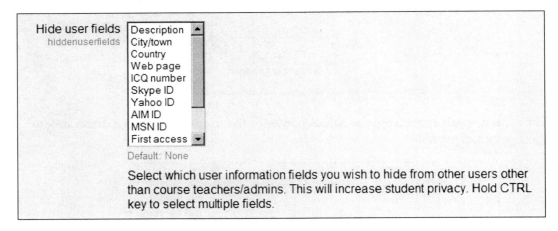

Using this approach you still cannot hide the user e-mail or his actual name which is good for cases where you want users to communicate with each other without knowing too many personal details.

Completely block ability to view profiles

If you want to completely block access to the user's profiles you have several options explained as follows:

Disable View participants capability

We already explained that by default every Moodle as of version 1.9.8 has this disabled by default. We are listing it here just for the sake of being complete.

Hide messaging system

Hiding messaging system means removing access points from user's reach. This means do not add Messages block on the front page and in any course where you wish to avoid users from knowing the other participants. This is useful where you want to have mixed messaging policy for different courses – set of users. Have in mind that this setup gives sort of a false sense of separation. Users from courses which do not have Messages block can still access Messaging system if they type the URL by hand.

Disable Messaging system

If you do not care for Messaging in your Moodle site you can completely disable it. To do that visit the **Administration | Security | Site policies** page and uncheck **Enable messaging system** option.

Not using general forums

If you have a website where you want to completely isolate only part of users within a course, among other things you can adopt the policy of not adding general forums inside such courses and on the site front page. That way you can still use forums in other courses where you do not have security concerns.

Disable View user profiles capability

If you want to completely block any possibility of viewing user profiles for specific role(s) you need to modify the View user profile capability and set it to "Not set". Visit the **Administration | Users | Permissions | Define roles** page, locate and modify that capability for every role you wish to prevent from viewing user profiles.

Course information protection

Protecting information contained within or related to the course is important. We will try to establish potential weak points in accessing course data and ways to eliminate them or at least reduce the exposure. This primarily focuses on course backups since they treat potentially sensitive user information.

Course backups

Moodle offers a possibility to create backups of your courses. This feature is essential in maintaining history of changes within a specific course and also offers safeguard against any potential errors or hardware crashes. You should be aware of the backup process in greater detail in order to better understand potential pitfalls and security problems that may occur.

During course backup process Moodle offers a possibility to choose which parts of a course we want to save. By default only users with Administrator or Teacher role can perform course backup. If user has `moodle/backup:userinfo` capability enabled then he will be able to take the backup of user data, user accounts and their role assignments within course, course activity logs, and user profile pictures. User data consists of all files submitted by users, forum posts, glossary entries, etc. Only Administrators have this capability enabled. Have in mind that this description applies to Moodle starting from 1.9.7.

Important information for users of Moodle prior to 1.9.7

In older versions of Moodle both Teachers and Administrators where enabled to perform full course backups with complete user information including hashed passwords.

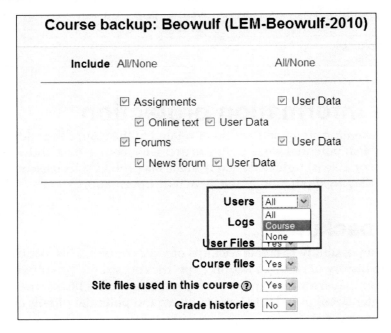

Password hashes and salt

In web applications passwords are almost never stored in clean text format since that is considered a security breach. To avoid storing such sensitive information directly developers usually hash passwords and store that value. **Password hash** is a result of deterministic procedure that takes an arbitrary block of data (in this case user password) and through specified mathematical process (hash algorithm) produces fixed size string.

Until recently it was established as sort of de facto standard to use MD5 hash algorithm for protecting passwords. It became so popular that various public hash databases appeared online like `http://www.md5decrypter.com/`. If somebody got a hold of a hashed passwords generated with MD5 algorithm he could pass them through one of these databases and possibly recover at least some of them. Have in mind that all these sites do not actually decrypt the hashed password since that is not possible. What they do instead is compare the hash against the previously stored list of known hashes, usually based on most common, insecure, password patterns like dictionary words, etc.

To make use of these sites obsolete developers started adding so called salt values. The **salt values** are randomly generated string of characters added to the actual password value prior to generating hashed value. Using this approach no MD5 decrypted site will be able to decode such hashed password.

Let us test this. For example, if we take a really insecure password `1234` and a random salt value of `$%#qw!`. These are the hash values we will have:

Password	Salt	Hash
1234		81dc9bdb52d04dc20036dbd8313ed055
1234	$%#qw!	e588c02025b2f1e3e7ca075804b1017b

If we go to the `http://www.md5decrypter.com/` and try both hashes these are the results we will have, first for unsalted hash:

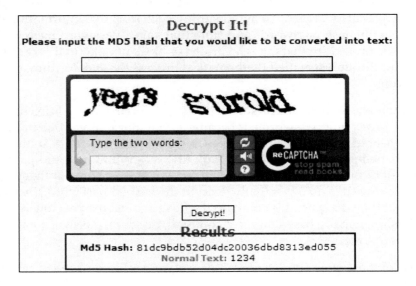

And then for salted hash:

Older versions of Moodle did not use password salt for higher password protection. Therefore, anybody with the hash database could easily break at least some passwords and thus illegally obtain access to the platform.

If you maintain Moodle instance prior to 1.9.7 then we strongly recommend you to do an upgrade. If that is not a viable option then do the following steps to secure your system:

Enable password policy

A password policy is a set of rules designed to enhance computer security by encouraging users to employ strong passwords and use them properly. Using such policies makes password theft much more difficult. To enable this feature visit the Site policies page and check the Password Policy option.

Enable password salt

Password salt increases the security of the generated encrypted password hashes, making a dictionary attack virtually impossible. This is done by adding a random stream of characters prior to the actual password before the hash is actually generated. By using this feature even if somebody obtains a course export it will be hard to get any useful data. See Chapter 1 for details on how to enable password salt.

Disable teacher's ability to back up and restore courses

In Moodle prior to 1.9.7, backup and restore of the courses was handled with three capabilities – `moodle/site:backup`, `moodle/site:import`, and `moodle/site:restore`. By default Administrator and Teacher roles had this enabled. Administrators should have this enabled but leaving this open to the Teachers may invite potential dangers. For example, a teacher could choose to export all user accounts in some course and then just by simply modifying a password hash for any user he would get access to those accounts once he imports the modified course backup again. To avoid this and other exploits, in the latest version of Moodle (1.9.7+) a teacher can only back up course data and cannot restore users (1.9.8+) even if they are present in the export. Since we cannot modify this behavior in older versions of Moodle the safest thing would be to disable these capabilities for the Teacher role. To do that visit the Define roles page (**Administration | Users | Permissions | Define roles**) and set the backup/restore/import capabilities to not set.

Backup courses moodle/site:backup	⦿	○	○	○
Import other courses into a course moodle/site:import	⦿	○	○	○
Restore courses moodle/site:restore	⦿	○	○	○

Security issues with course backups

Individual course backups—the ones performed from within the course are always stored within a default course backup directory. Default course backup directory is located in this path `<Moodledata path>/<course id>/backupdata`. Access to this directory is available to any user who has enabled `moodle/course:managefiles` capability. This is a case with Administrators and Teachers. You can access course file directory through administration block within course.

Imagine a situation where an administrator performs a manual single backup of a course and leaves the file without deleting it. Any user with access to this directory will be able to freely access this export. He can also download it, replace it, or even delete it! The best practice in this case would be to create a backup and move it to some location only accessible to the administrator thus effectively removing it from Moodledata or if the administrator does not have direct access to the server resources he could just download the generated backup from Moodle and then delete it on the server.

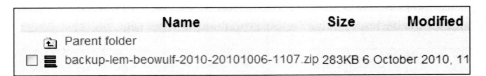

One way of preventing this would be to disable the access of the teacher to course files. This is not the recommended course of action as it would seriously cripple the teacher's ability to create courses. He would not be able to upload or link any file within a course. The real solution to this problem is to never store course backups within course directory. It effectively means that Administrator should never create backup from within a course. Backups should always be performed by scheduled backups utility.

Scheduled backups

Scheduled backups offers a possibility to execute batch backup of any course within your platform at any desired moment. This way of making safe copies of your platform structure also offer a possibility to store the actual backups outside the course directories. To configure this visit the **Administration | Courses | Backups** page and locate the **Save to** text field. In there set the path to an external folder somewhere outside your Moodledata directory.

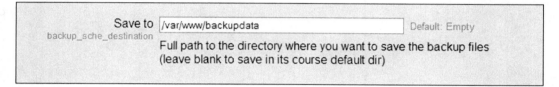

On Linux execute this to create such a directory:

```
/bin/mkdir /var/www/backupdata/
/bin/chown -R root:apache /var/www/backupdata/
/bin/chmod -R ug=rwX,o= /var/www/backupdata/
```

On Windows open elevated command prompt and execute this:

```
mkdir Z:\backupdata
icacls Z:\backupdata /Q /T /inheritance:r
icacls Z:\backupdata /Q /T /grant Administrators:(OI)(CI)(F)
icacls Z:\backupdata /Q /T /grant moodle:(OI)(CI)(F)moodle:(OI)(CI)(F)
```

You can use daily scheduled backup as a crash recovery strategy. You will be able to easily recover any course stored in the backup. Have in mind that this is very resource intensive operation, so choose wisely a time where you want to run it, preferably when you have low number of users accessing the platform.

Summary

We exposed some security issues related to the user information within Moodle and ways to resolve them. We explained what user information is available within Moodle and ways for other users to access it, with a detailed section that explains how to close or limit those points if that is what we want. We also talked about pitfalls related to the backup and how to restore the courses, explained the importance of having a proper password policy, and configured password salt. After applying recommendations from this chapter your Moodle site will be much safer and will expose only the amount of information that you actually want. In the next chapter we will talk about monitoring features within Moodle.

Monitoring User Activity

9

An administrator's work does not end with the installation and configuration of Moodle and the Operating System. Monitoring the server must be a regular part of service maintenance. If there is any problem in the way some part of the system works it can produce total loss of service or massive slowdown and thus prevent your users from accessing the website. In this chapter we will talk about ways of monitoring the status of Moodle and underlying OS components with the purpose of early detection and prevention of any kind of problems. The content is presented in the sections based on the tools and techniques available within Moodle or within OS:

- Activity monitoring using Moodle tools
- Activity monitoring using OS native tools

Activity monitoring using Moodle tools

Moodle offers several options when it comes to analyzing and monitoring user activity inside the platform. Monitoring is not real-time but it is close enough for most regular needs.

Moodle log

The word log has several meanings. The one we are interested in is defined as *a regular or systematic record of incidents or observations.* In computer terminology log is a place where some program stores a list of events that are intended for later potential review by an administrator. Log can be generated and stored in various places and formats. The most simple and common format is a plain text file. Every system should (and usually does) have some logging facility. That is also the case with Moodle. Since Moodle is a heavily database oriented application it was somewhat logical to implement its log inside the database. Log is stored in <table prefix>log table. In the version of Moodle used for writing this text we have over 290 locations where logging is performed. It covers all essential system operations like logging in, entering the course, various administrative tasks, etc. All this ensures that any administrator will have a rich and detailed set of data ready for the analysis.

Having the raw data is far from being enough for any simple and usable analysis. Fortunately, Moodle has several report views that utilize this information and present them in various formats. There are three global and two course level reports. All global reports can be also accessed from within the courses and in those cases they default their presentation to that course. We will focus only on the reports that have direct value for administrative purposes—Logs, Logs live, and Statistics. The remaining of the reports is more oriented towards Instructors and other educational staff. Viewing log is an important tool for detecting inappropriate behavior of some user. For example, if we notice that some user sends 150 forum posts in less than half an hour, then most likely we have a spam bot within a system and we should probably disable or delete such account.

Accessing the Moodle reports

Moodle reports can be accessed from two locations. One is site **Administration** block and another is the course **Reports** page. The Site **Administration** block is visible to any user with the administrative rights. To open the desired report, expand the **Reports** section inside the block and click on it.

Course administration block is visible to any user with permissions to administrate a course. It is usually located on the left side of the screen. To access the **Reports** page locate and click on the link with the same name.

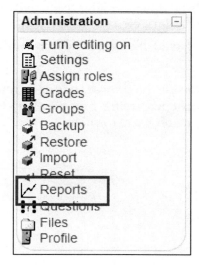

Logs report

The Logs report is a report that applies to the entire platform and also on a specific course level. It is probably the most important report for any administrator and because of that we will spend a bit more time explaining how it works. Every user action within Moodle is logged into a log table. That covers action like logging in, entering the course, opening a specific activity, etc. The log cannot actually tell us how long a user spent working on some activity due to the way the web application works but we can at least have a glimpse at the initial intentions.

In essence, the logs report represents raw data from the Moodle log table in the database. As a bonus it adds the possibility to filter the data based on several criteria:

- **Course**: User is permitted to choose either one specific course or the entire site data
- **Participant**: Moodle will present the list of available users that are present in the selected data time frame
- **Day**: User is offered a choice between one day from the history or the entire available data
- **Activities**: Using this field we can filter the activity on the particular activity type (forum, quiz, calendars, etc.)
- **User actions**: A list of available logged actions (add, update, delete, view, or all actions)

The result can be displayed inside the browser or can be retrieved in several file formats for storage or later post processing. Moodle offers text (CSV), ODS (Open Office spreadsheet), and Microsoft Excel formats.

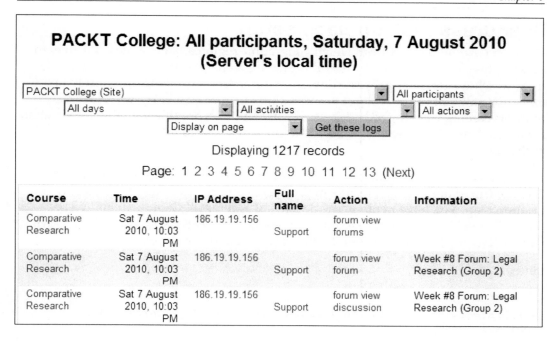

We will now explain the display format of the log report as follows:

- **Course**: Displays the full name of the course to which an action was executed. Name of the course is also a link, which we can click to visit the actual course.

- **Time**: Log time displayed in server local time.

- **IP Address**: IP address of the user who executed the action. IP address is taken from the user's browser header so it cannot be considered 100 percent correct or reliable. IP address itself is also a link that leads to the IP look up pop-up page.

- **Full name**: Complete name of the user who performed the action in case the user was logged in, otherwise it is empty.

- **Action**: Shows the name of the action performed and at the same time links to the element of the site or course to which it refers to.

- **Information**: Detailed information about the element upon which the user performed action usually name.

IP address look up page setup

Often it is useful to know from which geographic region a page request(s) came. In general this information can be useful for having general statistics of the access data from which we can later generate demographic charts. Also it is important to know this information if we are subject to some kind of cyber attack. We can block the requests coming from logged addresses easily and also provide valuable information for the forensics if and when we decide to present a case to the appropriate authorities.

To help us with this, Moodle offers integration with Google maps and the MaxMind GeoLite City datafile which results in producing a fairly accurate (99.5 percent) location map. You have to manually download and install GeoLite datafile. The recommended location of the GeoLite datafile is <Moodledata directory>/geoip. Here is how to obtain and install the file for Linux and Windows:

Linux:

```
cd /tmp/
/usr/bin/wget http://geolite.maxmind.com/download/geoip/database/
GeoLiteCity.dat.gz
/bin/gzip -d GeoLiteCity.dat.gz
/bin/mkdir /var/www/moodledata/geoip/
/bin/mv GeoLiteCity.dat /var/www/moodledata/geoip/GeoLiteCity.dat
/bin/chown -R root:apache /var/www/moodledata/geoip/
/bin/chmod -R u=rwX,g=rX,o= /var/www/moodledata/geoip/
```

Windows:

```
mkdir Z:\moodledata\geoip
bitsadmin /transfer getgeolite /priority HIGH http://geolite.maxmind.
com/download/geoip/database/GeoLiteCity.dat.gz Z:\moodledata\geoip\
GeoLiteCity.dat.gz
gzip -d GeoLiteCity.dat.gz
```

 Windows does not ship with `gzip` command-line utility. You can download it from the `gzip` home page—http://www.gzip.org/. There are also numerous programs that you can use on windows to unpack the `gzip` archive such as 7-Zip, WinRAR, WinZIP, etc.

Configuring Moodle to use GeoIP database

Final step is to configure Moodle to use GeoIP database. Open the **Administration | Location | Location** settings page and go to the **IP address lookup** section. Set the appropriate complete path to the GeoLiteCity.dat file according to your OS.

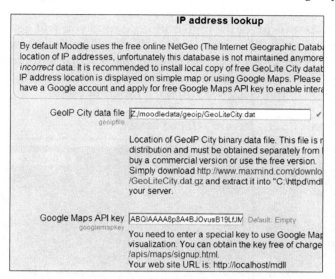

As a result of these changes you can now click on the IP address which will produce a pop-up window with IP information and approximate location on the world map.

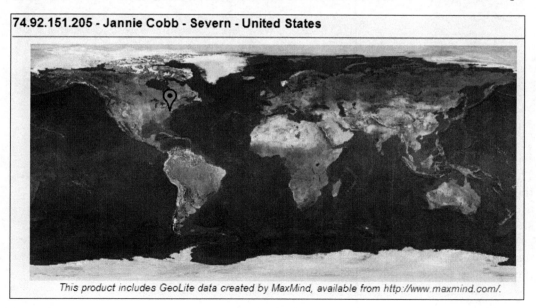

As an additional bonus Moodle also supports integration with Google Maps service which can produce a much more exact location map. This is quite useful for pinpointing exactly where the physical location of the computer that made a request is, and especially useful for the law enforcement units. To use that service you need to register for Google Maps API access. You can do that free of charge by visiting this site http://code.google.com/apis/maps/signup.html. To register you must have a Google account. As a result of the registration process you will get a special key (randomly generated string of 86 characters) which will be linked to your account and permit any software client to access Google Maps. Copy and paste that value into Google Maps API key box on the Language page and save the change. Now if we click on the same IP in the log we will see a different picture.

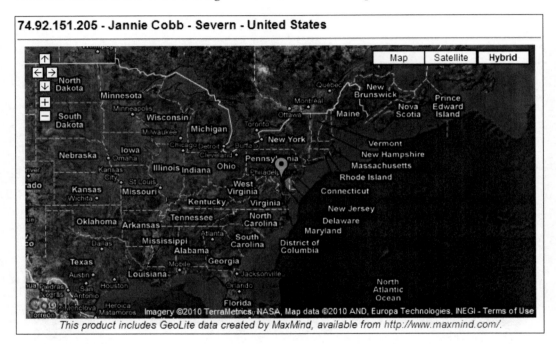

74.92.151.205 - Jannie Cobb - Severn - United States

This product includes GeoLite data created by MaxMind, available from http://www.maxmind.com/.

Live Logs report

This report is a slight variation of the Logs report. It displays only the records from the log table that were generated in the last hour. It is intended as a quick way to access the latest log data. It does not offer any filtering or sorting feature. Data is shown in the order they are generated. If accessed from the administrative block platform, it shows all log entries. On the other hand if you access it from the course it shows only the record related to that course. The report is always displayed in the new pop-up window that reloads its content every 60 seconds.

Statistics report

The purpose of this report is to offer general statistics about the user usage of a platform in general. Statistics are generated based on the log information. They are calculated during cron execution. Let us say few words about Moodle cron.

Moodle cron

Cron is a time-based job scheduler in Unix-like computer Operating Systems. The name cron comes from the word "chronos", Greek for "time". It is generally used to schedule administrative or maintenance tasks that need to be executed periodically without user intervention. Since the original development platform for Moodle was Linux it took a lot of terminology from that world. Moodle has its own task scheduler called cron, as the rest of the platform is implemented in PHP and enables periodical execution of various tasks crucial for the platform. We actually need to use OS task scheduler service to periodically execute Moodle cron.

Moodle cron on Windows

To setup periodical execution of the Moodle cron on Windows we need to use Windows Task Scheduler service. This is a template for a command you need to execute from the elevated command prompt in order to create the specific task:

```
schtasks /Create /RU moodle /RP <valid password> /SC HOURLY /TN "Moodle
cron" /TR "<path to php.exe> -c <path to php.ini> -f <Path to Moodle>\
admin\cron.php"
```

Or using our defaults from previous chapters it would look like this:

```
schtasks /Create /RU moodle /RP moodle /SC HOURLY /TN "Moodle cron" /TR
"C:\php5\php.exe -c C:\php5 -f Z:\website\moodle\admin\cron.php"
```

This creates a task that will be executed every hour. To see other options available open elevated command prompt and execute `schtasks /Create /?`.

Moodle cron on Linux

To set up periodical execution of the Moodle cron on Linux we need to use real cron service. CentOS 5 has several predefined locations for placing tasks that are executed periodically. They are all located in the `/etc` directory and their names start with cron followed by a time specifier, for example, `cron.hourly`, `cron.daily`, etc.

Open some text editor and create a file called `moodle.cron` with the following content:

```
#!/bin/sh
/usr/bin/sudo -u apache /usr/bin/php -f /var/www/moodle/admin/cron.php
```

Make sure that the file is located in one of the predefined cron directories—in this case we will use `/etc/cron.hourly`. After that, mark it for execution:

```
/bin/chmod u=rwx,go= /etc/cron.hourly/moodle.cron
```

Enabling statistics report

After all this is set up we need to actually configure statistics inside Moodle. By default statistics are not enabled. To enable that functionality we should:

- Visit the **Administration | Server | Statistics** page
- Check **Enable statistics** option and choose value for the **Maximum processing interval** option

> This option defines how much data from the log should be processed during the first run. The default setting is None. However, if you already have older log entries included into statistics, then you might want to specify a desired time span which can range from **1 week** to **All**.

Now you need to wait for at least one day for the cron to be executed to have the initial data for the statistics. Once all that is finished you can finally go to the **Administration | Reports | Statistics** page.

At first you will be presented with an empty page with several options, which you can choose before generating the report. The first option is **Course** which permits you to choose specific course for the statistics or the entire platform, and the second option is the type of activities you would like to see. They can be all activity, views, posts, or logins. Finally, you can choose the **Time period** for which you want your report to be generated.

After setting the desired values click on the **View** button. That will generate the report. A statistics report has one graph that shows the level of selected activities during given period of time. The same information used to generate the graphic in common table format is shown as follows:

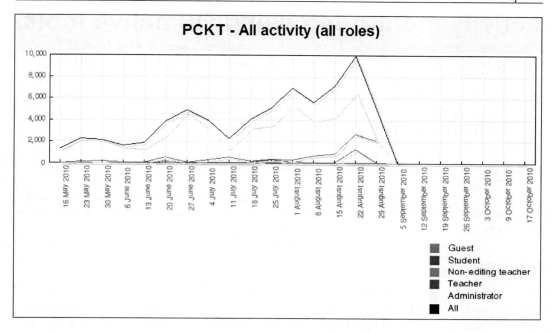

It is generally recommended to remove statistics for the courses that are finished and thus control the size of the log table. You can do this by visiting the **Administration | Server | Cleanup** page and set **Keep logs for** to the desired value. The value which you might choose here depends on the amount of traffic your site generates. The more active users you have the sooner the size of the log table will grow. We suggest keeping the logs for at least 90 days.

Activity monitoring using OS native tools

It is important to understand and know what condition your server is in at all times. This is important so that you can remedy any unwanted behavior quickly and prevent potential data loss. In this section we will focus on the tools that come already installed with the Operating System. Bear in mind that this is far from being a complete guide to the server monitoring. Refer to other books that talk about the administration of your specific Operating System.

Linux

In the following section we will present a few basic but quite useful Linux tools and services that can be used to monitor and determine the state of a particular service or resource usage.

Server load

There are quite a few tools that you can use to determine the status of the server. The first and most commonly used is top. This command is a part of every standard Linux distribution. To use it just open the command prompt and execute it under a user account that has administrative rights.

```
top - 12:23:58 up 11 days,  3:51,  1 user,  load average: 0.01, 0.04, 0.01
Tasks:  90 total,   2 running,  88 sleeping,   0 stopped,   0 zombie
Cpu(s):  2.0%us,  0.2%sy,  0.0%ni, 97.7%id,  0.0%wa,  0.0%hi,  0.0%si,  0.2%st
Mem:   1788724k total,  1777752k used,    10972k free,     1392k buffers
Swap:   917496k total,   143256k used,   774240k free,    94068k cached

  PID USER      PR  NI  VIRT  RES  SHR S %CPU %MEM    TIME+  COMMAND
28564 apache    15   0  535m 493m 2284 S  4.3 28.3  1:56.76 httpd
   92 root      10  -5     0    0    0 S  0.3  0.0  0:02.28 kswapd0
    1 root      15   0  2088  644  616 S  0.0  0.0  0:00.81 init
    2 root      RT   0     0    0    0 S  0.0  0.0  0:00.07 migration/0
    3 root      34  19     0    0    0 S  0.0  0.0  0:00.01 ksoftirqd/0
    4 root      RT   0     0    0    0 S  0.0  0.0  0:00.00 watchdog/0
    5 root      10  -5     0    0    0 S  0.0  0.0  0:00.05 events/0
    6 root      10  -5     0    0    0 S  0.0  0.0  0:00.00 khelper
    7 root      11  -5     0    0    0 S  0.0  0.0  0:00.00 kthread
    9 root      10  -5     0    0    0 S  0.0  0.0  0:00.00 xenwatch
   10 root      10  -5     0    0    0 S  0.0  0.0  0:00.00 xenbus
   19 root      RT  -5     0    0    0 S  0.0  0.0  0:00.04 migration/1
   20 root      34  19     0    0    0 S  0.0  0.0  0:00.00 ksoftirqd/1
```

Looking at the output you will see the list of all active processes, their ID's, users under which they are executed, the actual name of the command, and the amount of physical memory and CPU power consumed at that time. In our case the two processes that would be most interesting for us are web server, Apache (command httpd), and database server MySQL (command mysqld). The process list is constantly updated and it is therefore useful for real-time monitoring of server load. To see more information about this command execute man top.

Disk space

Knowing how much of the free space is left is an essential piece of information. To list global status for all existing partitions you use the df command. Execute the following from the command line:

```
/bin/df -Th
```

An example of the result is as shown follows:

```
Filesystem      Type      Size   Used  Avail  Use%  Mounted on
/dev/sda1       ext3      9.9G   4.2G   5.2G   45%  /
/dev/sdb        ext3      335G   784M   317G    1%  /mnt
none            tmpfs     874M      0   874M    0%  /dev/shm
/dev/sdf        xfs       250G    31G   220G   13%  /data
/dev/sdg        xfs      1000G   741G   260G   75%  /backup
```

You can use du command if you need to know how much space a specific directory or file occupies. For example:

```
/usr/bin/du -hs /var/www/
```

This will output the total size of that directory.

Web server load

Apache offers a special extension that permits an administrator to view CPU and memory load of the web-server itself directly from the browser. To configure this extension follow these steps:

1. Create a text file with following content:

    ```
    <Location /server-status>
        SetHandler server-status
        Order deny,allow
        Deny from all
        Allow from <put permitted IP or domain>
    </Location>
    ```

2. Save the file to the /etc/httpd/conf.d/srvstatus.conf.

3. Make sure to add the appropriate permitted IP or domain from which an administrator can actually connect.

4.. Now open the Apache configuration file /etc/httpd/conf/httpd.conf, locate the line with ExtendedStatus directive and uncomment it. The end result must have a line that says ExtendedStatus On.

5. Restart the web server.

6. After this you will be able to visit the page `<my server location>/server-status`.

The part of the sample output is as follows:

Srv	PID	Acc	M	CPU	SS	Req	Conn	Child	Slot	Client	VHost	Request
0-0	8599	0/3/3	_	0.00	14282	0	0.0	0.00	0.00	192.168.136.1	192.168.136.129	GET /favicon.ico HTTP/1.1
1-0	8600	0/3/3	_	0.00	10	1	0.0	0.00	0.00	192.168.136.1	192.168.136.129	GET /favicon.ico HTTP/1.1
2-0	8601	0/3/3	_	0.00	5	1	0.0	0.00	0.00	192.168.136.1	192.168.136.129	GET /favicon.ico HTTP/1.1
3-0	8602	0/2/2	_	0.00	14285	15	0.0	0.00	0.00	192.168.136.1	192.168.136.129	GET /favicon.ico HTTP/1.1
4-0	8603	0/2/2	W	0.00	0	0	0.0	0.04	0.04	192.168.136.1	192.168.136.129	GET /server-status HTTP/1.1
5-0	8604	0/2/2	_	0.00	14286	0	0.0	0.04	0.04	192.168.136.1	192.168.136.129	GET /usage/daily_usage_201011.png H
6-0	8605	0/2/2	_	0.00	14286	0	0.0	0.00	0.00	192.168.136.1	192.168.136.129	GET /usage/hourly_usage_201011.png
7-0	8606	0/2/2	_	0.00	14286	1	0.0	0.00	0.00	192.168.136.1	192.168.136.129	GET /usage/ctry_usage_201011.png H

Web server statistics

Apache produces an extensive access and error log that gets created every day. It is far from easy to read or understand this raw information. To be able to understand it we need some tool that can process and analyze that wealth of information. There are quite a few log analyzers available in the market. Some are free and others are commercial. With CentOS **The Webalizer** comes by default. The Webalizer is a fast, free web server logfile analysis program. It produces highly detailed, easily configurable usage reports in HTML format for viewing with a standard web browser.

Configuring The Webalizer

We need to check if The Webalizer is already installed. To do that, execute this from the command line:

```
rpm -qa | grep webalizer
```

If you get a full package name as a result (for example, `webalizer-2.01_10-30.1`), then that means it is installed, otherwise you need to install it. This is done by executing:

```
yum -y install webalizer
```

Once the package is installed we can proceed with the configuration. Inside the Apache configuration directory (/etc/httpd/conf.d/) we can find the newly added file webalizer.conf. By default it is configured to store webalizer reports into the /var/www/usage directory and to permit access only to the users coming from the same machine. That is probably too restrictive for general purpose usage. To fix this just add a new "Allow from" rule specifying your IP or the set of IP's from which you tend to connect from into webalizer.conf. Something like this:

```
<Location /usage>
    Order deny,allow
    Deny from all
    Allow from 127.0.0.1
    Allow from ::1
    Allow from .packt.com
    Allow from 10.1.0.0/255.255.0.0
</Location>
```

That is all the configuration we need to do. During installation of The Webalizer system already created cron job to update the web server statistics every day. It is called 00webalizer. For details see the file /etc/cron.daily/00webalizer.

As a final step restart the Apache web server and execute manually the cron job from the command line for the first time to generate some output (execute /etc/cron.daily/00webalizer). You can view the generated statistics by visiting <my website url>/usage.

This is an example output of one The Webalizer session:

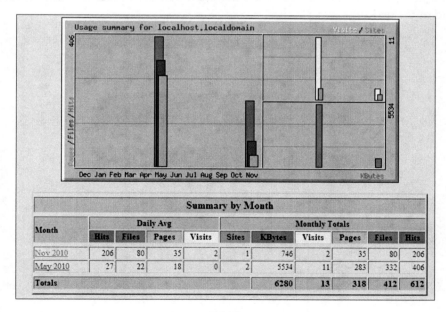

Month	Daily Avg				Monthly Totals					
	Hits	Files	Pages	Visits	Sites	KBytes	Visits	Pages	Files	Hits
Nov 2010	206	80	35	2	1	746	2	35	80	206
May 2010	27	22	18	0	2	5534	11	283	332	406
Totals						6280	13	318	412	612

As you can see you are presented with per-month statistics. You can then click on the specific month and see much more detailed day-by-day statistics together with IP information and pages that were requested by users.

If in case you have a shared hosting server or a server over which you do not have full control, these instructions do not apply. Contact your provider's technical support so that they can provide you with access to the traffic statistics.

Windows

In the following section we will present a few basic but quite useful Windows tools and services that can be used to monitor and determine the state of a particular service or level of resource usage.

Server load

On windows we can monitor server load using several tools. The most commonly used for quick preview would be the task manager.

Task manager

Task manager is an application similar in principal usage and intention to the Linux `top` utility. It is able to display all running processes and services together with their memory and CPU load. To start the task manager open **Run** dialog (**Start menu/ Run**) and enter **taskmgr**.

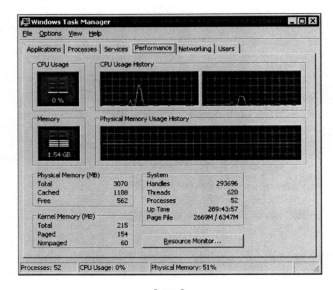

You have separate views (tabs) for types of processes like applications, all processes or services, performance overview, or network load. This utility is available on every version of Windows.

Performance and Reliability Monitor

Windows 2008 brought a lot of new tools that can help every administrator to monitor resource usage. The most important addition is renewed Performance Monitor. In this latest edition it offers more information than ever. To start this application use **Start Menu | Administrative Tools | Performance and Reliability Monitor**.

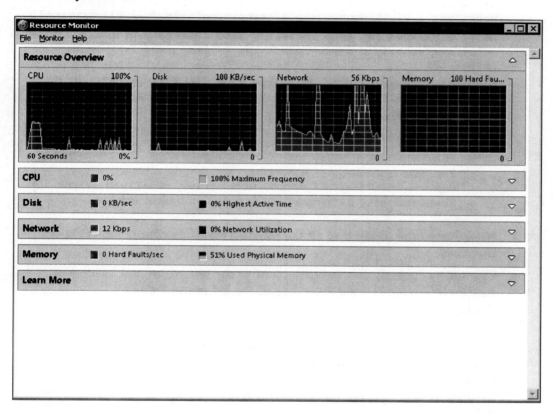

Four major server resources are presented with real-time graphs and separate sections below. Clicking with the mouse on a graph or section name will open or close the appropriate view enabling you to see more details.

The Webalizer on Windows

Configuring The Webalizer to work on Windows with IIS is a slightly more complicated but still possible task.

1. Visit the `http://www.webalizer.org/download.html` URL and download the available version for Windows (at the time of writing it was 2.21-02), latest GeoDB database, and country flags graphics for nice visual presentation. Here are the commands we will use to download everything:

   ```
   mkdir z:\temp

   bitsadmin /transfer getw /priority HIGH http://lt.rv.ua/wa/
   webalizer-2.21-02-cygwin.zip Z:\temp\webalizer-2.21-02-cygwin.zip

   bitsadmin /transfer getg /priority HIGH ftp://ftp.mrunix.net/pub/
   webalizer/webalizer-geodb-latest.tgz Z:\temp\webalizer-geodb-
   latest.tgz

   bitsadmin /transfer getf /priority HIGH ftp://ftp.mrunix.net/pub/
   webalizer/webalizer-flags.tgz Z:\temp\webalizer-flags.tgz

   mkdir z:\webalizer

   mkdir z:\website\moodle\usage
   ```

 The paths of the files we use here may change at the point when you decide to install the tool. Check the `http://www.webalizer.org/download.html` for the latest valid version of all three archives.

2. Now extract the contents of all the three archives into the `z:\webalizer` directory.

3. Open file `z:\webalizer\sample.conf` in the text editor and locate and modify following options according to the list presented here:

   ```
   LogType    w3c
   OutputDir       Z:/website/moodle/usage
   ReportTitle    My Moodle statistics report
   HostName   <put here your platform URL>
   GeoDB      yes
   GeoDBDatabase   Z:/webalizer/GeoDB.dat
   Quiet      yes
   TimeMe     yes
   CountryFlags  yes
   FlagDir    flags
   ```

4. After you have finished modifying the configuration file save it in the same directory with a new name—`webalizer.conf`.

The Webalizer can take log information either from the standard input or from a file specified in configuration. Unfortunately, IIS generates log files every day with a different name and for that reason we cannot use the configuration file. However, there is an option of creating a custom batch script file that can pass the correct information to The Webalizer executable. The format in which the IIS generates log filenames is `u_ex<2-digit year><day><month>.log`. This is what the script looks like:

```
@echo off
@set wlogroot=C:\inetpub\logs\LogFiles\W3SVC2\
@for /f "tokens=1,2,3,4 delims=/ " %%a in ('DATE /T') do set
mdate=%%b%%c
@for /f "tokens=1,2,3,4 delims=/ " %%a in ('DATE /T') do set
myear=%%d
@call set mmyear=%%myear:~2,2%%%
@set wlogfile=%wlogroot%u_ex%mmyear%%mdate%.log
@if exist %wlogfile% goto doit
:err
@echo %wlogfile% does not exist!
@goto end
:doit
@%~dp0webalizer.exe -c %~dp0webalizer.conf < %wlogfile%
:end
```

This script assumes that all logfiles are stored in `C:\inetpub\logs\LogFiles\W3SVC2\` which is the case for our setup but since the path on other systems will most likely be different, check and modify the value of `wlogroot` variable before actually using the script. Pass the content of this script to a new file located in `z:\webalizer` directory and call it `iis_webalizer.cmd`.

> Script uses the output of the command `date` to get the year, month, and date values. It is tuned to the US short date format in Windows 2008 command line which is `dd M/d/yyyy`. If your language and date format differs from the one we used here then you might need to modify part of the script that parses the date values.

Add a new scheduled task which will execute this script on daily basis, this time using this command line:

```
schtasks /Create /TN "Webalizer"
/TR "Z:\webalizer\iis_webalizer.cmd" /SC DAILY
/MO 1 /DU 02:00 /K /NP
```

You might have noticed that we decided to store the output of The Webalizer statistics in the existing directory where the Moodle itself is installed. This is to simplify the availability of the statistics to the admin. To access once generated statistics, just visit `<your moodle URL>/usage`.

Summary

We explored Moodle and OS native tools, services, and reports that can be useful in monitoring the system health and reacting accordingly. The reader was presented with a detailed explanation of Moodle log and the ways it can be used. We also presented Linux and Windows native tools that offer deeper insight in the status of various system services (free disk space, RAM usage, CPU load, and so on.). Finally, we explained how to install and configure native statistics tool for integration with the web server — The Webalizer. After all this you should be able to understand and maintain your server in a much better condition.

10
Backup

Backup is the cornerstone of every well maintained production server. This chapter will try to explain the importance of such procedures regarding Moodle and present tools available both within the platform and outside of it. We will also try to offer some guidelines for what to do in case of total server failure. This is the content outline:

- Importance of backup
- Backup tools in Moodle
- Site backup
- Disaster recovery scenario

Importance of backup

According to an online etymology, **dictionary backup** (or to be more exact back up) means *stand behind and support* or just *support*. The noun meaning of the same word is *reserve* or *standby*. The meaning specifically related to the computing could be expressed as *a copy or duplicate version of a file, program or entire computer system, retained for use in the event that the original is in some way rendered unusable.*

To help you understand better the importance of having adequate backup strategies, a simple fact is that any server will fail at some point. Failure can be caused by numerous reasons but all causes can be divided in two major groups—hardware failures and software failures. Hardware can (and at some point will) fail due to reasons like design flaws, poor production quality commonly viewed in new types of devices with less than perfect quality assurance process, or simple wear out that happens usually after a component has reached the end of its projected useful life. Software failures are even more common. It is estimated that all software has at least a moderate amount of bugs. There are more chances for existence of undiscovered bugs in the more complex software. In 2002 the **National Institute of Standards and Technology (NIST)** released the results of a survey showing that software bugs and errors cost the US economy USD 59.5 billion per year. All this shows that it is not only recommended to have backup strategy but it is an essential process in having and maintaining a production Moodle server.

As a web application Moodle consists of three crucial elements that must be backed up:

- Database
- Moodledata directory
- Moodle directory

You would also need to have clear and exact installation and configuration documentation that outlines the steps needed to setup your production server from scratch. But before going into all the details regarding that process let us see what Moodle itself offers in that area.

Backup tools in Moodle

Corner stone of every LMS is a course. Moodle is no different than the rest in that area. It offers a mechanism to backup, restore, or import individual courses. Every course can be backed up manually or automatically.

Manual backup

Manual backup can be performed from the course administrative block by clicking on the **Backup** option:

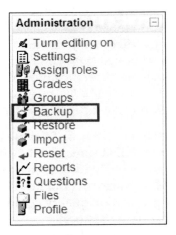

This leads us to the screen where we can choose which parts of the course we want to be exported. We will not go into much detail here since we talked about this in Chapter 8 and the screen itself is rather self explanatory. What is important to mention that all manual backups are always stored in course directory—<moodledata>/<course id>/backup.

As you already know we do not encourage use of manual backup procedure due to potential security issues. In case you need to perform manual backup make sure to move the exported course to a safe location as soon as possible. Safe location in this context means a directory not accessible to any of the course users.

Automatic backup

Automatic backup is a way Moodle creates a backup of all courses in a predefined time interval. It is a very useful option for keeping the course history changes. In order to use this option we need to configure it. Visit the **Administration | Courses | Backups** page. There is a multitude of options which you can use for tailoring the process to your specific needs. The first 11 options are related to the parts of course you may or may not want to back up. By default everything is disabled.

Content export options for automatic backup

Here is the quick list of recommended settings for the exporting options:

Option	Description	Recommended setting
Include modules	Backup course activities	Enabled
Include module user data	Backup data generated by users within activities	Enabled
Metacourse	Export all data from external courses too*	Disabled
Users	What users to export with course	Course
Logs	Export log entries related to the course	Disabled
User files	Export user files generated by users within activities	Enabled
Course files	Export files from course directory	Enabled
Site files	Export site files used within course	Enabled
Grade histories	Export grading history (enable only if you have grading history activated on the platform level)	Disabled
Messages	Backup user instant messages	Disabled
Blogs	Backup user blog entries (enable only if you actually use blogs)	Disabled

* Metacourse is a special kind of course that can embed two or more external courses. Enabling this option means that all inherited data from external courses would also be exported with Metacourse. Enable this option only if you actually use Metacourses.

Execution configuration options

The five options for configuring the backup process itself are as follows. We can specify when and where we want to create and store backups. Here is the list and explanation of the options available:

- **Keep**: This option is important because it enables us to specify how many backups per course to keep. By default it is set to 1. The number you choose should depend on several factors. What kind of server do you have? How much available free space do you have? What is the average size of course export within your instance of Moodle? How many courses do you have?

  Answering all these questions will help you determine the correct value for this parameter. If you are not sure, then start with the default value.

- **Active**: This one is simple and straightforward. You must enable it in order to actually use automatic backup. Have in mind that automatic backups are implemented as Moodle cron task. You must set up and enable execution of Moodle cron (for details see Chapter 9).

- **Schedule**: Determining an appropriate moment for executing backups is an important step in configuration of automatic backups. It actually depends on the pattern usage your courses have and it also relates to their number. The reason I'm mentioning the actual number of the courses is because the bigger and more complex the courses are the more server time and resources will be used during export.

Rant corner

Moodle backup is not well implemented because it has problems with handling big and complex course structures. This is especially true when quizzes are present. There were reported cases of backup process eating up more than several hundred MB of RAM or effectively crashing. This is the reason that backup and restore is largely rewritten in the upcoming Moodle 2.0. It promises to solve all these issues and offer moderate memory usage and a larger degree of stability.

Since backup is a memory and CPU intensive task it is essential to choose appropriate time of day for executing backup. Usually this would be between midnight and 3:00 a.m. This of course depends on the execution time set for the general Moodle cron. Here you can choose the days in the week where you would like to execute backup. We recommend selecting all days in the week if you have a sufficiently long low-usage time frame every day.

- **Execute at**: Here we select the actual hour at which the backup task will be executed. The default value is set to midnight. That is a good starting point. You can move to another hour that is more appropriate for your kind of setup.

When to use Moodle automated backup

There are several questions to which you need to give affirmative answer in order to know whether you can successfully use this tool.

- Can you successfully execute manual backup of every course?
- Do you have a sufficiently large platform low-usage time frame (at least one hour) for executing backup?
- Do you have enough free disk space on your server?

If answer is yes to all these questions you can consider using the automatic backup. If not you will have to focus on site backup procedures.

Course backups do not replace the usual site backups and should never be used as a primary backup system. They can be considered more like complements to the standard backup process.

Site backup

We already mentioned three crucial elements that must be backed up in order to have a safeguard against site crashes.

Database

Database backup consists of exporting database structure (tables) and data. Export can be in some proprietary format or as a standard SQL script. Since our focus was on MySQL database we will explain the process for that **Relational Database Management System (RDBMS)**. If you happen to use another RDBMS consult the vendor documentation for the appropriate export procedure.

MySQL comes with variety of command-line tools mostly for administrative purposes. The tool for exporting database is called `mysqldump`. This is a recommended template command line for exporting a single database from MySQL assuming that the command is being executed on the server where the database is running.

```
mysqldump -u<username> -p<password> --opt --result-file=<output file>
<database name>
```

Using our values for the Linux, setup export would look like this:

```
mysqldump -uroot -psomepass --opt -result-file=/tmp/moodle-export.sql
moodledb
```

Or in case of Windows:

```
mysqldump -uroot -psomepass --opt -result-file=Z:/temp/moodle-export.sql
moodledb
```

Now that we know how to manually export a database we need to automate this process and order it in a designated manner.

To automate database backup we need to create a script that will export the database and store it in a predefined location on the server. This is done through the usage of shell scripts. Windows and Linux use different shell scripts so we will present separate scripts for each Operating System. Before doing that we need to improve the actual command line for `mysqldump`. It is considered a security flaw if an administrator uses a command-line tool to access some password protected resource and places a password within the actual the command line. `Mysqldump` gives us an alternative for specifying options. They can be read from a separate configuration file. That way the only thing we must ensure is that the configuration file itself is well protected against undesired user access. This is the configuration file `my.ini` which we recommend for backup use with `mysqldump`.

```
[client]
default-character-set=utf8
add-drop-table=true
add-locks=true
comments=true
complete-insert=true
create-options=true
disable-keys=true
extended-insert=true
quick=true
quote-names=true
set-charset=true
single-transaction=true
dump-date=true
verbose=true

#this should be modified by user
user=<username>
password=<password>
#host=<host address>
#pipe=true
#socket=<socketname>
```

The section marked by the commentary for modification is the one you should be modifying to adapt to your own needs. If Moodle is installed on the same server where MySQL runs as is the case in this book, you only need to place the appropriate username and password.

 Make sure to use a database user that has backup rights. This means that you cannot use a DB user moodle that we created. You should use root account or create a new one and assign appropriate permissions to it.

Server log

Server log is a logfile or (several files) automatically created and maintained by system log server. It is used as a central storage for all activity events on the entire server. It is essential to review system logs on a regular basis. That can give you an early warning of any potential issues or offer an insight into a particular problem. In the following section we will give a brief explanation of log systems on Linux and Windows because all scripts in this chapter will write to subsequent system logs.

Linux

All Linux and UNIX distributions use Syslog as a standard server log implementation. There are several logfiles on a standard Linux and the one we are interested in is related to the applications. It is located usually at `/var/log/messages`. To see the latest events from the application system log execute the following command:

```
/usr/bin/tail /var/log/messages
```

If you want to filter entries you can use something like this:

```
/bin/cat /var/log/messages  | /bin/grep <filter word(s) >
```

Every entry in the system log has several elements like facility, event priority, tag, and description message. Facility is a generic category that identifies a source of an event. It can have values like daemon, cron, user, news, etc. Event priority states a level of importance of the event and it can be emergency, alert, critical, error, warning, notice, etc. Tag is a custom application set identifier that can be used to easily identify the entry. It is usually a single word. To add an entry into system log we can use logger command. Format of the command is as follows:

```
/bin/logger -s -p <facility>.<priority> -t <tag> <description message>
```

For example, executing this command will add an event entry into log:

```
/bin/logger -s -p user.err -t Moodle "Test error entry"
```

To see the actual event let us filter the log using the tag word we have chosen here — Moodle.

```
/bin/cat /var/log/messages  | /bin/grep Moodle
```

The outcome might look like this:

```
Nov 21 19:07:28 ip-10-212-155-65 Moodle: Test error entry
```

Windows

Windows has a different concept of system log. It is much more visually oriented. Log entries are called events. To access system events you can use event viewer. Event viewer can be accessed from **Start menu | Administrative Tools | Event Viewer**.

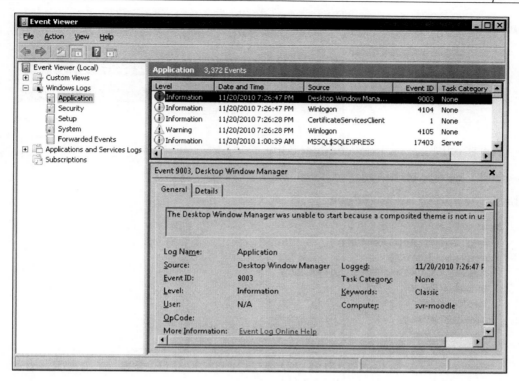

To create a custom event from a command line we can use `eventcreate` utility. It has the following format:

```
eventcreate /l <logname> /t <level> /so <facility> /id <event id> /d
<description>
```

Logname: Represents one of the available logs. By default it offers application, security, setup, system, and forwarded events. The one we plan on using in our scripts is application.

Level: Determines the type of event and can be error, warning, or information.

Facility: Is a custom identifier that describes an event source. It can be any text value.

Event ID: This is a numeric identifier that can have a value between 1 and 1000.

Description: Detailed textual explanation of the event.

Here is a command-line example:

```
eventcreate /l application /t error /so Moodle /id 1 /d "Test error
event"
```

And this is how the result looks in event viewer:

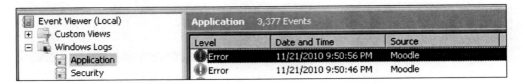

We can also list events from command line using `wevtutil` like this:

```
wevtutil qe application /rd:true /c:1 /f:text
```

This is the output we might get:

```
Event[0]:
  Log Name: Application
  Source: Moodle
  Date: 2010-11-21T21:50:56.000
  Event ID: 1
  Task: N/A
  Level: Error
  Opcode: Info
  Keyword: Classic
  User: S-1-5-21-3609673158-3230877478-3424243811-500
  User Name: SVR-MOODLE\Administrator
  Computer: svr-moodle
  Description:
Test error event
```

Automating database backup—Linux

To automate database backup we need to create a script that will export the database and add it to the cron execution list. At the same time we want to write the outcome of the execution into a system log. For a start create a new file `/etc/cron.daily/moodle_backup.cron` and put the following content inside:

```
#!/bin/sh
now=$(date +%d-%m-%Y)
backupcmd=/usr/bin/mysqldump
dbname=moodle
bckupdir=/var/db/backup
config=/etc/cron.daily/my.ini
archive=$bckupdir/dump_$now
logfile=$archive.log
backupfile=$archive.sql
scriptname=Moodle
```

```
successmsg=Backup finished OK!
failmsg="Unable to backup database! \
Checkout log file $logfile."
$backupcmd --defaults-extra-file=$config \
-r $backupfile $dbname 2> $logfile
rval=$?
if [ $rval -eq 0 ] ;
then
    /bin/logger -s -p user.info \
    -t $scriptname "$successmsg"
else
    /bin/logger -s -p user.err \
    -t $scriptname "$failmsg"
fi
exit $rval
```

Now create a `my.ini` file in the same directory and copy the content from the previous section. Do not forget to modify username, password, and other parameters specific to your installation.

We need to mark the new script as executable:

chmod u=rwx,gu= /etc/cron.daily/moodle_backup.cron

To finish the process we need to create a backup destination directory:

mkdir /var/db/backup

chmod u=rw,g=r,o= /var/db/backup

Backup script explanation

To really understand the backup script you will need a basic knowledge of Linux shell script also known as BASH script. If that is not the case just read on to learn what should be modified in case your distribution or general setup is different from the one presented here.

The first five lines of the script are variables that you may need to modify. It is explained as follows:

- Now: Contains the current date as textual value in the format day-month-year. You should change this only if you prefer a different date format. This text will be appended to export filename making it easily distinguishable from the rest.

- Backupcmd: Contains the location of mysqldump program. Modify it if your location is different from the current.

- Dbname: Name of the database you want to export, most likely you will have to change this.

- Bckupdir: Location where all backups should be stored. If your disk organization and/or preference is different than what we have presented here, modify this value.

- Config: Location of our custom my.ini file. Since we recommend placing the configuration file in the same location as cron script you should change it only if your cron file location differs from ours.

After every execution a logfile is created and preserved in the root backup directory. This is important for your information. Having an activity log can help you determine and diagnose any problem that might occur. Have in mind that you should periodically delete the old logfiles created by this script.

Automating database backup—Windows

Batch shell script in Windows is quite different from BASH but it is a required tool for any serious administrator that maintains a server with that OS. Create a directory called backup. In our setup it would look like this:

mkdir Z:\backup

mkdir Z:\scripts

Now open a text editor and copy inside the following content:

```
@echo off
@set backupcmd="C:\Program Files\MySQL\MySQL Server 5.1\bin\mysqldump.
exe"
@set dbname=moodle
@set now=%date:~4,2%-%date:~7,2%-%date:~10,4%
@set bckupdir=Z:\backup
@set config=%~dp0my.ini
@set archive=%bckupdir%\dump_%now%
@set logfile=%archive%.log
@set backupfile=%archive%.sql
@set successmsg=Backup finished OK!
@set errormsg=Unable to backup database ^
%dbanme%. Check %logfile%.

@%backupcmd% --defaults-extra-file=%config% ^
-r %backupfile% %dbname% 2> %logfile%

@if %errorlevel% neq 0 goto dberr
@echo %successmsg%
```

```
@goto end

:dberr
@echo %errormsg% 1>&2
@eventcreate /l application /t error ^
/so Moodle /id 1 /d "%errormsg%"

:end
```

Save it into `Z:\scripts\moodle_backup.cmd`.

Now in the same directory create a new file called `my.ini` and save the content presented in database section. Do not forget to modify the username, password, and other parameters specific to your installation. You can see that the basic structure of both scripts is quite similar. Differences are mostly related to the syntax of the two scripts. To see the explanation of the parameters you may need to modify the Linux section since all instructions expressed there also apply here.

As a final step create a scheduled task, which will execute this script every day. From elevated command prompt execute the following command:

```
schtasks /Create /TN "Moodle Backup"
/TR "Z:\scripts\moodle_backup.cmd" /SC DAILY /NP
```

Restoring database

Having backups is important but we also should know what to do in case we need to restore the database from the backup. First of all we should create an empty database and then perform the actual import. This is how it can be done from the command line:

```
mysqladmin -u<user> -p<password> create <database name>
```

And then the actual data import is:

```
mysql -u<user> -p<password> <database name> < <backupfile.sql>
```

In case you want to directly replace the existing database, the commands would look like this:

```
mysqladmin -u<user> -p<password> drop <database name>
mysqladmin -u<user> -p<password> create <database name>
mysql -u<user> -p<password> <database name> < <backupfile.sql>
```

To perform any of these tasks you should use administrative root user for MySQL or any other user with the same set of permissions.

Moodledata directory

This directory serves as file storage for all platform needs. It is essential to have it in order to maintain consistency of LMS.

You might think that backing up a single directory should not be a huge problem but it is actually a bit more complex than it looks. When we make a backup copy of part of the file system we would like to:

- Make sure we copied all files
- Make sure we copied all files correctly
- Make sure we transferred any specific permissions on all files and directories
- Keep the separate log of all items copied during execution
- Log any errors or discrepancies into the same log file
- Report backup outcome to system log for later review

There are many ways to perform a file backup on both Linux and Windows. We will present here the simplest possible approach using only the standard OS tools available. Our implementation will always perform a full copy of Moodledata directory. If that is not acceptable for your case due to disk space or other specific conditions you will have to implement your backup differently.

Linux

There are quite a few native tools for copying files on Linux, but we need one that is capable of not only copying files and directories but also that checks the integrity of the copied files. The tool that fits this description is **rsync**. Rsync is an open source utility that provides fast incremental file transfer. It supports transfers on the same server or between two different servers over network. That fact also presents it as a good choice as you can adapt backup script to a different type of backup easily.

[To learn more about rsync type man rsync in the command line or visit the official website http://rsync.samba.org/.]

The script itself is structured in a similar fashion as the backup one. Create an empty text file in /etc/cron.daily/backup_files.cron and copy the following content:

```
#!/bin/sh
now=$(date +%d-%m-%Y)
source=/var/www/moodledata
destinationroot=/var/site/backup
destination=$destinationroot/$now
logfile=$destinationroot/backup_$now.log
```

```
successmsg="Backup created in $destination"
failmsg="Unable to create backup! \
Check log file $logfile"
direrrmsg="Invalid output directory! \
Check $destinationroot"
scriptname=Moodle
if [ -d $destinationroot ] ; then
    echo "" > /dev/null
else
    /bin/logger -s -p user.err \
    -t $scriptname "$direrrmsg"
    exit 1
fi
/usr/bin/rsync -av $source $destination &> $logfile
rval=$?
if [ $rval -eq 0 ] ; then
    /bin/logger -s -p user.info \
    -t $scriptname "$successmsg"
else
    /bin/logger -s -p user.err \
    -t $scriptname "$failmsg"
fi
exit $rval
```

The only things you should modify in this script are the values of variable source and destinationroot. Variable source should contain a full path to the Moodledata directory as it is on your system and destinationroot should contain a full path to the location on disk where you plan on storing all your backups. Let us create that directory:

mkdir /var/site/backup

Each backup will be stored in a sub directory named after a current date. We use a format day-month-year. The script first checks if the destinationroot directory exists and if it does not then an error is reported. If the directory check goes well rsync starts a copy of Moodledata directory. A logfile is created in <dirroot>/ backup_<date>.log file and it will contain all the output made by rsync during the backup process. You can use this information to review what was copied or not. After backup is finished, the script checks the general status of the execution. The result of that inquiry is reported to the system log. We mark all log entries in the system log with Moodle so you can use this command to filter all the backup entries from the log:

/bin/cat /var/log/messages | /bin/grep Moodle

If you place the script in the `/etc/cron.daily` directory as we suggest here, it will be executed every day at midnight. If that does not suit your needs you can check the cron documentation and create a custom schedule for your backup task.

 A fairly decent documentation about cron can be found on Wikipedia at `http://en.wikipedia.org/wiki/Cron`.

Windows

Although it is possible to set up and use rsync on Windows it is not a straightforward and simple task. Fortunately, Windows has xcopy utility that can copy the entire directory structures, transfer permissions, and verify file integrity.

Create a new empty file `Z:\scripts\backup_files.cmd` and copy the following content:

```
@echo off
@set now=%date:~4,2%-%date:~7,2%-%date:~10,4%
@set source=Z:\website
@set destinationroot=Z:\sitebackup
@set destination="%destinationroot%\%now%"
@set logfile="%destinationroot%\backup_%now%.log"
@set successmsg=Backup created in %destination%
@set failmsg=^
Unable to create backup! Check log file %logfile%
@set direrrmsg=^
Invalid output directory! Check %destinationroot%
@set scriptname=Moodle
@if not exist "%destinationroot%" goto desterr

@xcopy %source% %destination% ^
      /e /v /k /x /i /y ^
      1>%logfile% 2>&1

@if %errorlevel% neq 0 goto copyerr
@echo %successmsg%
@eventcreate /l application /t information ^
 /so "%scriptname%" /id 1 /d "%successmsg%" > NUL
@goto end

:desterr
@echo %direrrmsg% 1>&2
@eventcreate /l application /t error ^
```

```
  /so "%scriptname%" /id 2 /d "%direrrmsg%" > NUL
@goto end

:copyerr
@echo %failmsg% 1>&2
@eventcreate /l application /t error ^
  /so "%scriptname%" /id 3 /d "%failmsg%" > NUL

:end
```

Now create a destination directory for the backups:

mkdir Z:\sitebackup

As a final step create a scheduled task that will execute this script every day. From the elevated command prompt execute the following command:

schtasks /Create /TN "Moodle site Backup"

/TR "Z:\scripts\backup_files.cmd" /SC DAILY /NP

The structure and logic of this script is almost identical to that of Linux. Major differences are related to the actual syntax and specific tool names. To adapt the script to your setup modify the value of variables source and destinationroot. The script checks if destinationroot directory exists and in case it does not then backup is not performed and error is logged in the system event log. The actual backup is performed by xcopy that takes care of all the checks and validations. All execution process log is stored in <destinationroot>\backup_<date>.log file — Z:\ sitebackup\backup_<date>.log in our case. You can use this file for reviewing the actual outcome of the backup. After backup is finished, the script checks the general status of the execution. The result of that inquiry is reported to the system event log. Use the event viewer to check the actual outcome.

Moodle directory

There is generally no need to back up Moodle directory every day. You should make a manual backup whenever a new module is added/removed or upgraded or when you update the entire core. Make sure to place Moodle backup with appropriate database backups since quite often during minor versions upgrade database gets updated. If you still want to automate this task you can use the same scripts for Moodledata. Just change their name and modify the source and destination variables.

Disaster recovery scenario

At some point you might have a serious server crash that will force you to perform a full restore of your Moodle. Here is the list of steps you should take in case you apply the advice from this book:

1. Install and update your operating system. Reinstall the existing server with the same version of the operating system and prepare all disk partitions.

2. Install all needed system software (web server, PHP, database server) and configure it according to the recommendations in this book.

3. Restore the Moodle backup from your backup storage to the designated web directory.

4. Restore the latest Moodledata from your backup storage to the designated location on the disk.

5. Restore latest database backup into database server.

6. Check Moodle config and update the values for database connection (dbuser, dbpass, dbname) and location of Moodledata directory if different from the original.

7. Test the system to verify if it works correctly.

Summary

In this chapter you learned some basic things about backup and monitoring of Moodle dedicated server. After applying the things learned here you should be able to create complete and regular backups of your LMS and thus ensure and increase reliability. We are at the end of our journey. I hope you enjoyed it as much as I did. Some additional notes and information can be found in the Appendix. Any feedback from you, positive or negative, is more than welcome. Let me know what you think. Meanwhile I hope your Moodle will be safer and more stable after reading this book. Cheers!

Authentication Plugins

In this appendix we will present the remaining list of the other authentication modules that are shipped with Moodle and which were not discussed in Chapter 4.

Plugins less common in production servers

These plugins are all disabled by default in a new installation of Moodle and are not so common in everyday usage. We are presenting most of them for informational purposes.

LDAP server

LDAP (Lightweight Directory Access Protocol) is an application protocol for retrieving and modifying data from the directory service. LDAP server is often used as a source of user information. For this plugin to work, you will need LDAP and OpenSSL plugin for PHP. To make the connection as secure as possible, use LDAPs protocol. That way no interception will be possible. Also try to have a failover server because when the central server is down no user will be able to enter into the platform. In order to be able to use secure LDAP we need to make sure that OpenSSL and LDAP PHP extensions are installed and properly configured. We have already explained particular configuration bits of OpenSSL for both Linux and Windows, so let us focus on LDAP extension.

Configuring LDAP PHP extension

In general most of the configuration of the LDAP extension is located in a separate configuration file called `ldap.conf`. By default on Linux PHP looks for this file in `/etc/openldap/` while on Windows in versions of PHP before 5.3 default folder is `C:\openldap\sysconf`. In PHP 5.3 up to version 5.3.2 the default folder was a root of disk partition on which web server's main web documents folder is located (does that sound complicated or what?). As you can see PHP looks in various places for this file depending on various factors. What we want is to have a predictable way of placing and configuring location of `ldap.conf`. This is done by specifying environment variable `LDAPCONF` with the valid location of our `ldap.conf`. On Linux we should open Apache configuration file `httpd.conf` and add this line to it:

```
SetEnv LDAPCONF "<path to ldap.conf>"
```

On Windows we should set it up in the same place we defined `PHPRC` and `OPENSSL_CONF` (see Chapter 3 dedicated to configuration of Windows server).

After this configuration is applied we should restart the web server.

CAS server

CAS (Central Authentication Service) is a **Single-Sign-On (SSO)** system that enables the account linking of two or more different systems. By default this system requires HTTPS connection, so no particular additional configuration is needed within Moodle in terms of security other than what is already being mentioned in the first section of Chapter 4.

FirstClass server

FirstClass is proprietary groupware software mostly used by educational institutions to offer enhanced electronic communication and collaboration to their students.

IMAP server

IMAP (Internet Message Access Protocol) is one of the two most prevalent protocols for email retrieval. IMAP server can also be used as a source of user credentials. Often these servers use LDAP as their user back-end. In order to make access to this resource in a secure manner it is recommended to use encrypted protocol (IMAP Cert or IMAP SSL).

Moodle network authentication

MNET authentication is a plugin intended for a SSO with another Moodle instance. This instance is considered as a central user repository. This connection uses xml-rpc protocol over HTTPS and it is quite secure by default.

NNTP server

This plugin enables usage of **NNTP (Network News Transport Protocol)** for retrieving user information.

No authentication

This plugin disables authentication checking and in general should not be used in production sites.

PAM (Pluggable Authentication Modules)

This plugin supposedly gives support for PAM provider. However, it uses a PHP4 library which is no longer publicly available. Therefore usage of this module is not recommended for production sites.

POP3 server

This is another popular protocol for e-mail retrieval. In order to use this integration we recommend use of SSL connection with certificates.

Shibboleth

Shibboleth is another SSO solution (similar to CAS). In general it is safe enough for general usage.

Radius

Radius is a networking protocol that provides support for centralized Authentication, Authorization, and Accounting management for connecting and using network resources. Radius protocol does not transmit passwords in clear text and it implies usage of shared secret for connection validation.

Summary

We briefly presented a list of authentication plugins not so widely used with Moodle and explained a few configuration caveats and offered some recommendations.

Index

C

D

E

F

NNTP server 177
no authentication plugin 177
non-editing teacher, Moodle roles 82

O

OpenSSL plugin 175
options, Moodle security overview report
  administrators 22
  allow EMBED and OBJECT 20
  backup of user data 22
  default course role 22
  default course role (global) 22
  default role for all users 22
  displaying PHP errors 19
  email change confirmation 21
  enabled .swf media filter 21
  frontpage role 22
  guest role 22
  insecure dataroot 19
  no authentication 20
  open to Google 21
  open user profiles 21
  password policy 21
  password salt 21
  register globals 19
  writable config.php 22
  XSS trusted users 22

P

PAM 177
password hash 131
password policy 133
password salt 133
permissions
  about 80
  allow 80
  not set 80
  prevent 80
  prohibit 80
PHP
  about 33
  adding, to IIS 52
  installing 33, 34
  non thread-safe version, downloading 50
  non thread-safe version, installing 50

php.ini
  configuring 51
Pluggable Authentication Modules. *See*
      PAM
POP3 server 177
protection measures
  applying 109
  file upload, enabling in forums if needed
      109
  WYSIWIG editor, disabling if not needed
      109

R

Radius 177
rate posts 86
recursive acronym 33
Red Hat Enterprise Linux 5 server 24
Relational Database Management System
      (RDBMS) 162
risky capabilities
  backup user data 89
  change own password 88
  change site configuration and allowed to do
      anything 88
  configuration 87
  create new blog entries 88
  create users on restore 88
  privacy 87
  spam 88
  view participants (course level) 89
  view participants (system level) 89
  XSS 87
role
  about 81
  customizing 82-84
  overriding 85-87
rsync 170

S

salt values 131
search engine content indexing, Internet
      bots 91
search engines 91
security, Windows
  about 41
  anti-virus 44, 45

PUBLISHING community experience distilled

Thank you for buying
Moodle Security

About Packt Publishing

Packt, pronounced 'packed', published its first book "*Mastering phpMyAdmin for Effective MySQL Management*" in April 2004 and subsequently continued to specialize in publishing highly focused books on specific technologies and solutions.

Our books and publications share the experiences of your fellow IT professionals in adapting and customizing today's systems, applications, and frameworks. Our solution based books give you the knowledge and power to customize the software and technologies you're using to get the job done. Packt books are more specific and less general than the IT books you have seen in the past. Our unique business model allows us to bring you more focused information, giving you more of what you need to know, and less of what you don't.

Packt is a modern, yet unique publishing company, which focuses on producing quality, cutting-edge books for communities of developers, administrators, and newbies alike. For more information, please visit our website: www.packtpub.com.

About Packt Open Source

In 2010, Packt launched two new brands, Packt Open Source and Packt Enterprise, in order to continue its focus on specialization. This book is part of the Packt Open Source brand, home to books published on software built around Open Source licences, and offering information to anybody from advanced developers to budding web designers. The Open Source brand also runs Packt's Open Source Royalty Scheme, by which Packt gives a royalty to each Open Source project about whose software a book is sold.

Writing for Packt

We welcome all inquiries from people who are interested in authoring. Book proposals should be sent to author@packtpub.com. If your book idea is still at an early stage and you would like to discuss it first before writing a formal book proposal, contact us; one of our commissioning editors will get in touch with you.

We're not just looking for published authors; if you have strong technical skills but no writing experience, our experienced editors can help you develop a writing career, or simply get some additional reward for your expertise.

Moodle Administration

ISBN: 978-1-847195-62-3   Paperback: 376 pages

An administrator's guide to configuring, securing, customizing, and extending Moodle

1. A complete guide for planning, installing, optimizing, customizing, and configuring Moodle

2. Secure, back up, and restore your VLE

3. Extending and networking Moodle

Science Teaching with Moodle 2.0: RAW

ISBN: 978-1-84951-148-3   Paperback: 386 pages

Create interactive lessons and activities in Moodle to enhance your students' understanding and enjoyment of science

1. Follow a sample course to see how lessons, groups, and forums are created

2. Make your student's homework more exciting by enabling them to watch videos, participate in group discussions, and complete quizzes from home

3. Simplify the teaching of difficult scientific notation using animations

4. Monitor your students' progress using Gradebook

Please check **www.PacktPub.com** for information on our titles

Moodle 2.0 First Look

ISBN: 978-1-849511-94-0   Paperback: 272 pages

Discover what's new in Moodle 2.0, how the new features work, and how it will impact you

1. Get an insight into the new features of Moodle 2.0

2. Discover the benefits of brand new additions such as Comments and Conditional Activities

3. Master the changes in administration with Moodle 2.0

4. The first and only book that covers all of the fantastic new features of Moodle 2.0

Joomla! Web Security

ISBN: 978-1-847194-88-6   Paperback: 264 pages

Secure your Joomla! website from common security threats with this easy-to-use guide

1. Learn how to secure your Joomla! websites

2. Real-world tools to protect against hacks on your site

3. Implement disaster recovery features

4. Set up SSL on your site

Please check **www.PacktPub.com** for information on our titles

Lightning Source UK Ltd.
Milton Keynes UK
09 March 2011

168902UK00001BA/2/P